Also by George Boelcke:

It's Your Money: Tools, Tips and Tricks to Borrow Smarter and Pay it off Quicker – U.S. Edition

¡Quédese con su dinero! : los secretos del crédito y la deuda : lo que tiene que saber, lo que necesita evitar
(Keep Your Money – Spanish Edition)

The Canadian Financial Nightmare (Audio CD)

The American Financial Nightmare (Audio CD)

Colorful Personalities: Discover Your Personality Type Through the Power of Colors

Colorful Personalities: Audio CD

The Colors of Leadership and Management

The Colors of Sales and Customers

The Colors of Relationships

The Colors of Parent & Child Dynamics

Colors Tools for Christians

(all titles available through:www.vantageseminars.com)

It's Your Money!

*Tools, tips & tricks
to borrow smarter
and pay it off quicker*

Vantage Financial Consultants Ltd.
George J. Boelcke, CCP
Box 4080
Edmonton, AB Canada
T6E 4S8
Web site: www.yourmoneybook.com
E-mail: george@vantageseminars.com

This book and the information contained herein is intended as a general guide only. The author assumes no responsibility for errors, omissions, inaccuracies or any inconsistency herein and makes no promises or claims regarding the application or usage. The reader should always consult a financial professional for specific application to their individual situation.

Actual examples used are taken from newspaper advertisements and their terms, conditions, rates, rebates, prices, fees or any other factors may have been amended, terminated or materially changed. While great care has been taken in the preparation of all reference charts, they are a guide only and some are rounded to the nearest dollar. Specific payments should be obtained from the company you are dealing with.

THIRD EDITION

National Library of Canadian Cataloguing in Publication

Boelcke, George J., 1959–
        It's Your Money! Credit & debt: tools, tips & tricks to borrow smarter and pay it off quicker / George J. Boelcke.

Includes index.
ISBN 978-0-9734479-1-0

        Consumer credit. 2. Finance, Personal I.Title.

        HG3701.B63 2004   332.024   C2004-902725-5.

Design assistance: David Macpherson
Edited by: Crystal Lidgren
Layout & typeset by: Ingénieuse Productions, Edmonton

Printed and bound in the United States of America

It's Your Money!

Tools, tips & tricks to borrow smarter and pay it off quicker

An invaluable Reference Guide and must-read for every Canadian

George J. Boelcke, CCP

Contents

Introduction

Why You Need to Know

Credit—love it or hate it—most of us can't live without it. Unfortunately, most of us also don't understand it very well and that costs us dearly in the added interest we pay and total debt it accumulates.

This book should become your best friend, and should be your inside guide into many areas of credit. Having a basic knowledge of the what and how of credit is an invaluable resource for obtaining it, keeping it and then getting rid of it as fast as possible. You'll also understand your options, because anyone uninformed, in a hurry, unwilling to ask questions or easily intimidated, will never obtain the best deal for themselves. Let's face it, nobody has a vested interest in explaining shortcuts, savings or options to you.

Understanding the ins and outs of financing is a mystery to most people. There is no black or white answer and credit decisions are not mathematical equations with clear or tidy explanations. Credit decisions are as unique as the people applying, and sometimes that's very confusing. In the time it takes to read the next couple of pages:

- Dozens of Canadians will be filing for bankruptcy.

- Hundreds are signing mortgage papers, trusting but not really knowing, what their rights or interest charges really are.

- Thousands will be buying consumer goods on credit without knowing all the facts of what they're signing.

- Tens of thousands are charging away on their credit cards hoping, but not certain, to make more than a minimum payment next month.

- Hundreds of thousands are making payments on the purchase or lease of an automobile on terms that might have seemed a good idea at the time.

- Millions of individuals are carrying more than one credit card in their wallet and treating it as cash, with many potential pitfalls.

Every day, countless numbers of consumers make poor or uninformed credit decisions that create consequences for years to come. It is never by choice, but because they don't know the credit tricks or pitfalls, or the right questions to ask.

 The greatest asset you have is to ask questions—the right questions.

How did we get here and how do we avoid some of these expensive traps? It will be through understanding the inside rules and tips of credit—"how to get it"—in the least costly way. It is also through managing debt—the "how to get rid of it" part.

Obtaining credit is not a gift or a windfall as it only creates spending power for today. The downside is that repayment must be made at some point. This results in spending more money later when interest charges are added to make up for the "gotta have it today" attitude. So, it is always at a cost of future purchasing power when the bills arrive. When you're making payments on last year's stuff, you're using up a lot of money that can't be saved or put towards this year's stuff.

This book is not about numbers—they are deliberately kept to a minimum—even all examples are rounded to the nearest dollar. Plus, nobody expects you to read this book from beginning to end, but it will become an invaluable reference guide. You'll see many examples of ways you've borrowed without always knowing what's really happening with long forms, tiny print and pushy salespeople in your face. Chances are you might not have known what to look for, or to avoid, anyway—and who wants to look or feel stupid? Next time, you'll be ready—with some tools, knowledge and the right questions to ask. After all, if you don't ask nobody will, as others won't be making your payments or help with your debts.

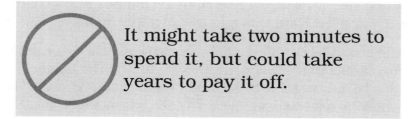

It might take two minutes to spend it, but could take years to pay it off.

As average Canadians, we owe over 115 percent of our disposable income in debts—and it's rising. At the same time our savings rate is between zero and minus one percent—ouch! For most of us it'll be years before we see the light at the end of the tunnel. More and more borrowing with an increasing debt load and almost no cushion of savings to fall back on is not a good combination. So for many Canadians, being debt-free is quite an unrealistic goal for the foreseeable future, and many are just a paycheque or two away from serious financial problems.

Chapter 1

The Start of Credit

Credit has been around for centuries. The word comes from the Latin credo meaning "belief", or simply put, "I trust". Documents date back to around 1800 BC when the King of Babylon referred to the granting of loans and punishment for any non-payment. The concept of interest came from Roman law and simply reasoned that charging interest (extra charges for making the loan) was a fair return to lenders.

Credit is broadly classified into two main areas. The first category is mercantile trade, which involves credit between businesses. In this field, being able to get credit is almost mandatory. Very few businesses could survive on a cash basis in their dealings with suppliers, customers or wholesalers. It has always been accepted that over 90 percent of transactions between businesses involve credit in some way.

Consumer credit is the same principle, but applied to individuals. It ranges from mortgages to credit cards, personal loans and lines of credit to overdrafts and pawnbrokers. It allows consumers the chance to buy now - pay later. Often a very tempting idea, but it comes with the responsibility of some planning and budgeting and can make the word credit misleading – perhaps the proper term should be taking on debt.

The other common theme is that most consumer credit involves borrowing for consumption, whether it's charging a meal, a new wardrobe, or borrowing to finance a boat or vacation. In all instances, the item is consumed or depreciates (reduces) in value. In other words, it's used up, gone or worth less down the road. That's quite different from credit obtained for investments, RRSPs or some asset that increases in value over time and where interest may even be tax deductible. That is actually borrowing money to make money.

The first widespread consumer credit was by Singer Sewing Machines. Their marketing was directed at women, who in that era were almost exclusively housewives. Selling sewing machines to them presented a problem, as the women were unable to afford it since they didn't possess much of their own disposable income. So Singer overcame this by creating a sale with a partial down payment and the balance paid over a number of months on affordable terms.

The second breakthrough came from the Ford Motor Company. With the advent of the automobile, Henry Ford also had the challenge of selling enough cars to customers who could not afford the entire price. His concept was similar in using a combination of down payment and monthly installments over a deferred period of time.

Since the end of the Second World War consumer credit has exploded and evolved significantly. It has played a huge part in the growth of the entire economy and created higher standards of living. Things such as credit cards and personal credit lines, as well as overall reductions in the amount of down payments have all left their mark. Some the for better – some for the worse.

Is credit really necessary or is it wiser to always pay cash? If the enjoyment of having something today through financing outweighs the cost, to that person it's worth it. However, it is quite normal to exaggerate the need at the moment, while often ignoring the cost or implications for the future.

Using credit might be convenient, but it always comes at a price. Whether that cost is worth paying only you can decide.

In spite of the natural tendency to downplay debt loads, credit sales drive a large part of today's economy. Without it, purchases of expensive ticket items would drastically decrease, as only those with sufficient savings could ever afford to pay cash. Credit is now an integral part of society. It allows individuals to enjoy a high standard of living and is essential to the operation of governments and all companies. One of the most fundamental elements in the production and movement of goods and services is to encourage consumption. Credit is also a field of constant changes and demands, and has evolved to computerized credit checks, instant approvals, automated collection systems and behaviour scoring.

Chapter 2

Credit 101

 Credit is something you must be able to manage well and use to your advantage—not just as a convenience.

Obtaining credit is not a right, but an earned privilege to be able to use the money of others. It involves the exchange or sale of goods and services for the promise to pay it back over a period of time and involves two main elements:

- Future - The time frame until the repayment is due or the length of time the money is owed.

- Risk - The chances of being paid back within a certain time as agreed to or being paid back when the loan is due.

Both of these are what lenders use to calculate how much interest to charge – how long the term is and how much risk there is in getting paid back. After the loan is made, the debt has to be repaid. If this does not happen, many will suffer to various degrees. Default on a credit card can impact all cardholders through higher interest rates at some point. On the other extreme, non-payment by large corporations or developing nations has a much larger effect throughout the economy.

Credit in everyday life can mean that ten dollars lent to a friend for a day is relatively risk free and a small amount. Another safe bet is $200 lent for a week while holding a $700 watch, since the collateral is more valuable than the loan. Borrowing in a more formal way from a financial institution operates much the same. A mortgage with a house as security will always have a lower interest rate than a finance company loan with or without collateral.

Credit and a credit rating is almost a necessity nowadays, as society continues evolving to become more and more cashless. No, not everyone has to have a credit card, or even wants one, but those people are few and far between. Without some form of plastic in your wallet, some lifestyle adjustments or inconveniences may be necessary.

It is very difficult to find anyone that doesn't rely on credit in one way or another. Even those that claim to only deal in cash actually deal with a form of credit. Since the abandonment of the gold standard, governments across the world continue to print money that they have to make good on. This paper currency incurs debt for the government, so paper money is also a form of credit. Another, is simply having a bank account. The depositor is really extending credit to the financial institution. It is a debt that has to be paid back to the depositor when the money is withdrawn. Financial institutions simply take the deposits of customers and recycle them by lending this money out through loans, mortgages and other forms of credit. They pay interest to customers with deposits and savings, while collecting fees and interest from lending out the money to others at a higher rate.

The What and How

For better or worse, today's society almost mandates having a credit rating of some kind. Seldom, if ever, will a car rental company release a vehicle without a major credit card and even just reserving a hotel room can be a challenge without one.

Obtaining credit is largely based on your past track record. Since someone is selling you credit in the hope of getting it back, it is their choice to say yes or no. Your option in the transaction is to shop around for the best terms, lowest rate and most favourable arrangements. The two goals for financial institutions are to lend out money at a profit and to be certain they get paid back. Large numbers of people think that creditors have a crystal ball and should be able to see that 'things are great now' that they should 'take a chance on me.' Simply put – it doesn't work like that.

 Credit is something you buy, while someone else gets to decide if they actually want to sell it to you.

What was the last big-ticket item you purchased? A computer, stereo or maybe a DVD player? Perhaps you checked a couple of ads or a few stores to find the best deal. You weren't always looking for the least expensive one, but probably a combination of features and price. Well how much time did you spend shopping around the last time you applied for a credit card, loan or mortgage? That same shopping could save you hundreds or thousands of dollars. Even a relatively small $20,000 vehicle loan over five years will save you almost $1,000 if you are able to negotiate a two-percent lower rate. Isn't that a worthwhile investment of time as well?

Payday Loans - The Short-term Credit Business

It is estimated that around 20 percent of the population has challenges getting credit for one reason or another. The main ones include lack of income, credit problems, total debt, or people who have simply fallen through the credit scoring cracks, have never fought back and just gave up. A large group of them find that a lack of job stability or minimal income, both of which are often related, make obtaining credit almost impossible. One alternative is a subprime interest rate at huge rates and often with many fees. The other is often the short-term credit industry. In all cases, the majority of lower income, or marginal credit applicants do get treated noticeably worse. When credit is granted, the prices and/or rates will almost always be higher than those available to other customers.

Every day there are ads promoting short-term borrowing until next payday. Unfortunately, these are very expensive and targeted to consumers with credit problems or the working poor. While it may sound easy, there are huge interest charges to pay for the convenience. This industry includes payday loan companies, pawn shops and other cheque-cashing operations. Many will advance up to 30 percent of an individual's net pay until the next payday. This emergency cash does come at a price – a very high price of up to 90 cents per $100 per week. Rates can reach more than 500 percent when interest is added to the fees and loans are rolled over (extended).

This industry is finally receiving some attention from Ottawa and a number of provinces have begun to implement more stringent regulations as well as rate and fee limits for this industry.

Payday loan companies generally charge posted rates of 59 percent, in addition to their fees, which is just below the legal limit set by the Criminal Code, but they are not always enforced uniformly. Their main business is the one-time repayment instead of a typical monthly payment plan. Customers leave a post-dated cheque or sign an automatic bank withdrawal for repayment on their next scheduled payday. Not being able to pay often leads to rolling over their debt by continuously arranging new advances to repay older ones, often with no end in sight. With vast numbers of operations, it is a highly competitive field. Their success is due to customers who are not well informed and the terms are not easily understood to an average borrower. They are the   fastest growing segment of alternative financing but only regulated in five provinces.

Unfortunately, these individuals often have nowhere else to turn for their financial needs. In fact, while Winnipeg MP Pat Martin calls these operations "an epidemic of the seediest form of financing that we used to call loansharking", he does acknowledge that in his riding alone, 14 bank branches have closed while over 20 short-term operations have opened in the past number of years. An apt description for an industry which markets loans to families who can least likely afford these loans and are forced to pay huge fees and interest just to stall off repayment until next payday.

The First-Timers

Yes, there are individuals who have never borrowed and have never desired a credit card. This is a small minority, generally older people, not raised with the concept of borrowing for any reason. Perhaps it's sad that it is something few people can accomplish these days. Today, prices in relation to income earned make it almost impossible to obtain certain things without some form of credit.

The underlying premise for credit decisions is a credit rating. Only by judging how someone else has been paid in the past, can any decision be made about the future with some degree of accuracy. To make matters harder to understand, the previous amount borrowed enters into this equation as well. It is referred to as the high credit and is a factor in almost all decisions. In simple terms, it means that someone with a department store credit card and a limit of $500 will not likely be approved for a $10,000 loan. The jump is simply too large to borrow 20 times more than ever before.

Credit is granted when the applicant has a good payment history. It is someone without excessive debt and the ability to repay the amount borrowed. This makes it important to establish a credit rating immediately upon reaching legal age. Learning about credit as a tool and a resource should not be something that is avoided until absolutely necessary. For better or worse, it is an integral part of today's society. And yes, building up credit can cost fees and interest charges. Paying some of these is a worthwhile investment in building a solid credit foundation. Any teen that has been taught at home about credit, both the pitfalls and benefits, will more likely be responsible and educated enough to ask good questions and take the right steps to successfully manage credit during their lifetime.

There are some common ways for first time borrowers to establish credit. These are based on the applicant being employed and with sufficient income to pay back the loan. Also,

85% of teenagers have never taken a course on credit or finance.

the assumption is that the applicant is of legal age and has no previous credit problems - having no credit is still better than bad credit.

- Department store card – Will generally approve first time applicants for a limit around $500. It may not be much, but it's an excellent start. They are easier to obtain as the merchant uses their in-house cards to attract customers. At the same time, it creates loyal clientele for them and increases repeat business.

- RRSP loan – Yes, this does count as a real loan. Most offer them at prime interest rates, as there is large competition to attract clients. Some will even process these loans in as little as five minutes. In return, the RRSP stays in their control until the loan is paid in full. This is an excellent way, with very little interest, to create a win-win situation of establishing credit and saving taxes while building savings for retirement.

- Someone else signing – This is the most common first loan for young people. A cosigner is someone that signs along with the applicant. That person becomes as equally responsible for the repayment and total debt as the actual borrower. Cosigners will always be asked to make payment in the event of arrears. That's why lenders tend to require a family member instead of a friend. Consequently it should always be considered as the last resort. Often a smaller loan or an increased down payment can eliminate the need for a cosigner. After all, would a family member prefer to lend someone an additional down payment or sign for the entire length and amount of the loan?

• Car loan – Assuming it's a reasonably priced used vehicle, a 30 to 50 percent down payment through a reputable dealer may well secure financing without a cosigner. No matter what, it never means higher interest rates, but only that the loan is structured to shorten the term or increase the down payment – both of which reduce risk. Vehicles need to be less than seven years old to qualify for decent rates.

• Secured Visa or MasterCard – Some financial institutions issue these specialized credit cards and a list of most is at the back of the book. Secured means a cash deposit in the amount of the credit limit is placed on deposit as collateral against any potential non-payment. Other than this deposit, the card looks and charges exactly the same as any other. The amount stays in place until the credit card is closed or changed to a regular card. This is an excellent method of obtaining good credit references after 18-24 months.

• Loans secured with a term deposit or G.I.C. – Any loan that is fully secured is fairly easy to obtain. Would you lend someone $100 if they gave you a $100 to hold as collateral? Of course - sounds stupid? - not really. The term deposit or G.I.C. may be locked in or attract interest penalties if cashed early. Besides, a little interest paid on a loan while getting most of it back on the term deposit is a worthwhile investment, and an easy solution to build a good credit rating.

• Student credit cards – For years now, card companies have aggressively marketed to college or university students. Statistics show that the default rate, or rate of serious arrears, is not significantly higher than average. Some even claim "Applying for a Visa Card is as easy as writing your own name. You don't need a cosigner. You don't need a job. After all, being a student is your job." The reason they are prepared to do this? Studies in the U.S. have shown that three out of four college students stay loyal to this first card for more than 15 years.

For students it is worthwhile to graduate with a credit rating as well as a degree.

They are relatively easy to obtain and establish the foundation of a good credit rating. 65 percent of students do have a credit card, but almost 40 percent also carry a balance. In fact, almost one-fifth of students actually have a balance over $3,500. While it may seem like a good idea at the time, it is also creating a potential financial nightmare. Before your son or daughter gets his or her own credit card, have them watch a movie called, *Maxed Out.*

All of these options have some basic common denominators. The credit extended is of a relatively modest amount, or has a large down payment. Secondly, the credit grantor is quite secured for the amount of the funds advanced. This is done either by holding collateral in cash, term deposits or through a large equity percentage in something like a vehicle because of the down payment. Both reduce any risk to the credit grantor since nobody is likely to walk away from that type of arrangement.

Chapter 3

Credit Cards

 If you eat it, wear it, drink it or put it in your gas tank— don't charge it. A new shirt or dinner out is never a good reason to incur debt.

Credit cards really got their start at the turn of the century when some innkeepers started to issue identification cards to their regular clients. They were meant to check in and out, and allowed billing of charges by mail after the client had left. It's ironic that today without one of these now called credit cards, the chances of obtaining a room these days are next to none.

The first card useable at more than one establishment was Diner's Club, designed exclusively for restaurants in the early 1950's. Frank McNamara, the creator, signed up less than 100 members from his first mailer, but two years later was billing out over one million dollars and the credit card business was firmly established forever. Talk about a concept that was quickly accepted and is here to stay. Back then as is the case today, any personal touch was already long gone. The rows of computers with billions of transactions and millions of accounts made each cardholder simply a number – a long number – and one of very many.

With the massive costs of setting up and administering a credit card program, plus a learning curve that caused millions of dollars in write-offs, it became obvious in the late 1960s that only two companies of any size would survive. They removed any reference to charge or debit in advertisements, and Chargex became Visa, MasterCharge became MasterCard, and both started to evolve into financial service companies instead of simple credit card issuers.

At first, banks actually had little interest in credit cards. It was the desire to eliminate cheques that changed their minds. At one point, more than two-thirds of the entire economy's transactions (and 90 percent of all payments) were processed through cheques that involved massive amounts of labour and paperwork. Processing billions of little pieces of paper became a very expensive undertaking. There were also over a dozen steps for the banks that ranged from the acceptance of these cheques to the eventual return with the customers' statement and all the handling necessary in between. This inefficient system cost the banks many millions of dollars in administration costs, not all of which could hope to be recovered from customers through service charges.

Credit cards became their bridge from the use of cheques, to their eventual goal of electronic banking. A sort of training ground for customers to wean them off cheques and onto little plastic cards. The third was to get into a fast growing area that was becoming very lucrative and easy for them to compete in because of their massive client base. They started finding homes in Canadian wallets in the summer of 1968, and two years later were already being used to the tune of eight billion dollars without much prodding.

The first advertisements revolved around the themes of saving you time and hassle, and banks were well on the way to becoming an indispensable bank in everyone's wallet. They also kept pointing out that now you could take advantage of sales between paydays and the convenience of only one easy cheque to write for the balance each month.

It wasn't that hard to sell, and all that remained was some marketing fine-tuning. The large majority of charges are too small, disposable or perishable for actual loans. In other words, without these credit cards, borrowing for dinners, liquor purchases, clothing, gas or a host of services would not be possible. In frequently used ads for MasterCard, they refer to their card as 'smart money', quite a leap from calling it a charge card. Old habits die hard and most people tend to be creatures of habit. Very effective advertising campaigns have totally revolutionized and changed our view of money and cash. It has also radically re-defined our definition of debt and purchases.

> *"Our performance is a testament to Visa's business model as we continue to lead the migration from cash and checks to electronic payments."*
> Visa CEO Joseph Saunders

By 2008, total worldwide credit card charges had reached nearly seven trillion dollars. Today, credit card marketing continues to be a numbers game. The more apply, the more are approved, and the more people will carry big balances and pay huge interest and fees each month. That's why it's hard to walk from one end of a mall to another without being pitched that just filling out an application can get you a free T-shirt or other valuable gift.

Almost any conventional lending requires collateral of some kind or another. Not so if someone can simply use two, three or four credit cards that may easily add up to $10 or $20 thousand of totally unsecured debt – for anything at any time. How many cards are too many? At one point, Walter Cavanagh certainly had the record with over 1,300 valid cards. Yes, he was rejected once – only once – when a store suggested he already had a sufficient number. You think?

 Unfortunately a frequently heard comment is: "I can't afford it, so I'll just put it on my credit card."

Just in Visas and MasterCards, there are now 64 million cards in Canadians hands with the average adult carrying more than four, a number steadily rising year after year. The numbers are much more staggering in the United States where the average adult carries over twice as many, with more than one billion in circulation.

Today, credit cards can seem more valuable than cash. It can be for retailers where the amount of money paid by credit cards far exceeds cash sales. In 2008, they were used for more than $240 billion in charges at an average amount of over $111.

More than 600 institutions market Visa and MasterCard that can be used at over 1.1 million businesses. Consumers can even pay insurance, parking, rent or their cell phone bills by having them charged to the card of their choice. Card issuers have almost perfected lending in reverse with the massive use of credit cards in the economy. Only then can they tack on interest charges ranging from 10 to 29 percent for the almost half of all accounts that carry an outstanding amount at the end of the month.

Any loan or mortgage requires repayment in a fixed manner. Quite the opposite is true with credit cards. Statistics in Canada show that only half of all credit card balances are paid in full each month. It's a sad day for the companies when their customers do pay off their balance. To avoid this as long as possible, even the minimum payments have now been reduced to three percent per month.

> *"The card was never intended to encourage*
> *people to spend beyond their means."*
> Joe Titus – First Credit Manager of The Diners Club (1959)

A better quote came from a past Visa USA President, Dee Hock: "People don't suddenly get dumb because we give them a piece of plastic." Well, Mr. Hock – maybe not permanently dumb, but sometimes...

 Research shows over and over that consumers spend almost 20% more on a credit card than they would with cash—always.

Card Categories

Credit cards are identified by four main categories:

- Major cards include Visa, MasterCard and American Express, which are certainly very extensive in their usage, quantity in circulation and acceptance worldwide.

American Express has a number of cards that operate differently than the two above. Their billing system requires payment in full by the due date. These "real" American Express cards are referred to as charge cards since they must be paid in full with each statement. Perhaps not a bad idea to be forced to do that each month.

- Affinity Cards: These are credit cards issued together with non-profit groups that have their name and logo on the cards. When they are used, a portion of the card volume goes to support that group or cause, generally one half percent at most. But should a $25 donation to the Elvis Presley Foundation, your University, or Ducks Unlimited on $5,000 of charges get anyone excited?

- Co-branded Cards: These are issued for specific companies such as General Motors, Staples and even Starbucks. They create a tie-in between the card and the merchant designed to keep their customers loyal. The tie-ins generally include points or rebates toward products of that merchant. General Motors, for example, has their tie-in with TD/Canada Trust for Visa cards and the opportunity to earn rebates towards the purchase or lease of a new vehicle. Not to be outdone, even VW is now marketing their own rewards card.

The latest ones? E-Bay has released a new co-branded card with MBNA to earn points towards purchases on their website. Also now available is a WestJet MasterCard, a Mike Weir MasterCard targeted to golf enthusiasts and a Staples Rewards MasterCard.

- Retail Cards include everything from gas stations to department store chains, stereo stores and furniture retailers. Since they are restricted to the establishment that issues them, they are very limiting but encourage customer loyalty to a certain retailer. These cards are either operated by the company directly, by a finance company or independently administered. Almost all financing through retail stores now comes with a credit card to allow further charges without another application at that particular retailer.

Convenience cheques are available with every major credit card. They are cheques to allow instant access up to the full credit limit. It is a quick way for the issuer to get customers maxed out and unable to pay their balance in full. It is something that would take a lot longer if it could only be done through purchases. They are first sent out with the intent of getting customers to transfer other balances over to the new card. That may be the case, but also allows customers to play a shell game between credit cards in using one to pay the other. Plus, these original balance transfers are generally treated as cash advances. The fine print will disclose that this means no interest free period, often at a higher rate, and they do not qualify for any introductory rate.

Credit card debt can become a mortgage for life, especially with the ability to get cash advances and access to convenience cheques. Interest on cash advances also has no grace period and starts immediately. On top of that, many issuers charge a fee, often $7.50 or more, for each cash-advance. In fact, over $34 billion in cash advances went through credit cards in 2008 alone and the annualized interest rates are staggering.

Stephen Markson, a former MBNA card holder, actually sued the company over two cash advances he took for $100 and $200, which he repaid within a few days. In the Ontario Divisional court, expert witnesses testified that these cash advances had an effective interest rate of over 94 percent.. But again, it is your option to stop the cash withdrawal feature on any card. It just takes a little discipline and a two-minute telephone call and shredding those cheques designed to drive up your debt.

 People with debt problems often blame credit cards. But isn't the real issue poor money management?

Credit Limits

All credit cards come with a pre-set spending maximum called the credit limit. It is the highest amount of money the card issuer is prepared to advance. Just as joint bank accounts have only one balance, credit cards have only one aggregate limit. No matter how many actual cards are linked to a dependent or spouse, the limit exists for all cards together. As there is only a single account, these supplemental cards as they are called, are the same account with different names. There is only one billing (plus one credit rating for the actual cardholder only) and one spending limit.

Once every year or two, it is likely there will be an increase in the credit limit. This might seem flattering, but they're trying to get you to load up enough of a balance where the hangover will last past the grace period. In other words - where the balance is not paid in full. With about half of all customers, that's already happening. Your job is to avoid it – their job is to get you to the largest balance with the least amount of default risk. Simply stated: Push it – but not too far. They still want to get paid back - just not very fast. There is still the annual fee for most, but they'd rather have your interest as well.

A few years ago card issuers also implemented another new U.S. style fee for going even one dollar over the credit limit.

The full chart of these is one page 185, however it averages over $20, which can be charged every month, or every time the balance is over the credit limit. This makes it critical to never get near the limit to avoid this fee designed to profit from those who can least afford it.

Why and How They Change

After setting an initial limit, the card issuer has no obligation to ever raise the amount. They can leave it, lower it (as has now become prevalent in the U.K. and U.S. because of the economic downturn) or increase it. After all, the card is the property of the issuer who can also cancel it. However, companies do adjust limits from time-to-time. Even the credit card field is a competitive marketplace with each company fighting not only for market share, but to retain their portfolio of well paying accounts. It is, as in any business, less costly to maintain a current customer than to attract a new one.

Credit limits are not set in stone figures. The issuer bases the starting limit on the original application. The amount is set by the issuer based on your credit bureau report and credit scoring. Everyone can most likely think back to his or her first major credit card. The limit at that time was likely in the $500 to perhaps $1,000 range. That same card today could well be a $3,000 limit or higher. Since the issuer has not updated the credit application, (nobody has called you to update any information) how did the credit limit get adjusted?

This is accomplished through something called behaviour scoring. In simplified terms, it deals with the conduct of the cardholder and can adjust credit limits based on this information. It's something made possible through the use of sophisticated computers and vast amounts of past data for each account.

A portion of this system reviews the usual amount of each charge. While the national average is $111, customers use them in different ways. The company's analysis can include information ranging from the number of charges each month, the average amount or the average monthly-unpaid balance. It can also gather information from each transaction regarding the type of purchases and much more. When this is included, it allows a certain degree of tailoring of credit limits to client needs. Having the card activity history available is simply good marketing and monitoring, but is also very valuable for fraud protection. Computer systems can quickly detect unusual charge activities – either in terms of quantity or amounts where the charge pattern has suddenly changed for a specific account.

How to Change Your Limit

Each customer has direct control over his or her card limit. It is simply a matter of contacting the financial institution to request a change. Information on the file is then updated and reviewed.

On the other hand, a customer can also decline an increase in a credit limit or simply lower the amount. Not all people should have a growing credit limit. Very few take this step, however it can be a great idea for people that:

• Previously consolidated credit card balances into a loan as the balances got carried away or unmanageable, if the card has not been returned or the account closed already.

• Are not comfortable in trusting themselves not to use the credit limit to the maximum.

• Maintain they only have the card for identification or emergency use.

• Recognize that a credit card, and high credit limits, are not status symbols. It is simply a convenience card that should only be used to the amount that can be comfortably budgeted and paid in full by the due date.

• Taking the step of reducing a limit is not a sign of a problem, or derogatory in any way, but just wise credit management.

Out of money? Stop spending! But with any number of cards and high limits, where is the reason or incentive to stop?

Annual Fees

In the early 1980s, inflation was running close to 20 percent and interest rates went up right along with it. In the US, President Carter and the Federal Reserve wanted to shift some of the blame to banks for rising rates. To slow down their use, they implemented a nine percent growth rate. Since the banks had no desire to limit profits, they simply began charging an annual fee and/or increasing the fees merchants had to pay for honouring the card (usually from one and a half to four percent). Bank of America was one of the first to institute an annual fee. To them, even if 10 percent of their customers cancelled, they were still collecting an extra 10 million dollars for doing nothing extra. From that point on, while perks may have been added, annual fees for most cards were here to stay. Not every card charges an annual fee. Many basic cards don't and some even waive it, if you ask, and if the card usage is high enough.

Every credit card accomplishes their basic purpose. After that, it comes down to an individual decision of finding the choice of features, benefits, rate, points or perks. At the end of the book is a listing of many credit cards with their issuer, minimum limits, points, fees and rebates. It's a very competitive field, so it always pays to shop around as the programs can certainly be amended, plus the rates and annual fees can also change from time-to-time. As a rule of thumb, cards with fees always include more features. But then it is always wiser to decide why you are getting the card in the first place.

Chasing Those Perks, Points and Rewards

These days, the majority of card holders are enrolled in some kind of reward program or another. Most are Gold cards that do come with some perks and benefits, but also with high annual fees. Card issuers love these cards and market their loyalty programs very aggressively. After all, once someone is enrolled, they tend to justify charging more and more on their card, pay those annual fees forever, and stay loyal to the card much longer than other clients.

Yet most people will likely never see any significant perks at all and do all of the charging but not much of the rewarding.

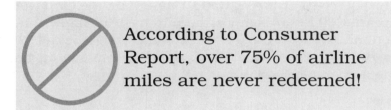
According to Consumer Report, over 75% of airline miles are never redeemed!

Before choosing a reward program it is important to understand that it will take quite some time, and a ton of charges, to get to any meaningful reward level. It is also important to read the fine print of how points are accumulated, what the annual fees are, understanding that redemption levels can change without notice, and are usually wiped out if the balance is ever in arrears.

One popular and heavily-marketed card is a travel card that promises "you can travel right away." Before you pack, however, here is the breakdown of the point accumulation using an example of a $1,000 free airline ticket:

Enrollment bonus of 15,000 points (with a $225 value, disclosed in the ad). It shows that each dollar spent on the card earns 1.5 cents towards free travel. For this card, the annual fee is $140.

A $1,000 ticket divided by $0.015 per dollar charged equates to $67,000 of credit card charges required to reach that free travel amount. If you are charging $500 per month, it will take more than 11 years to earn that free trip and those 11 years have cost a total of $1,540 in annual fees. Even at $1,000 in monthly charges it takes until the sixth year and cost $840 in fees.

Another example is the new Staples MasterCard which earns reward points towards store purchases. The bold print shows earning rewards up to 2%. It does not, however, explain what the "up to" entails, nor is there any disclosure of interest rates in the entire brochure or application. It took a 10-minute call to obtain the rate (19.9%) and breakdown of the point tiers: At $3,000 to $7,000 of annual volume, earnings are one percent, and only at $15,000 of charges does it reach the two percent. Charging $500 a month on the card would only earn $60 towards any retail purchase at Staples. More important, how few people would actually make the call to get rates, details and calculate their potential earnings or the time-frame needed before signing up?

The Free Grace Period

The grace period is the length of time from the date of your statement until you have to make a payment or pay the balance in full. On partial payments, interest on purchases will then start retroactive to day one if the entire balance is not paid. If the statement is paid in full, there will never be an interest charge on new transactions. For cash advances or convenience cheques, interest always starts from the date you take the funds – they are treated as a loan and have no interest free period. The grace periods can range from two to three weeks and are also outlined in the back of the book. It should be one of many considerations when shopping for a card as this free time can vary widely. For anyone determined to pay the balance in full, this extra week or so can certainly be worthwhile.

Does your interest free period stop just short of payday? This can be very expensive and isn't well known to millions of cardholders. It means you will be charged interest at the end of the grace period, for that full month, even if you pay only one day after the cut-off. So if you want the grace period to go until your paycheque arrives, contact your card issuer to change your statement date. For example:

Statement cut-off is   8th of each month
Grace period of   20 days
Interest starts on the   29th

If you get paid the last day of the month and pay your balance – it's still too late; the interest has been charged, as you have not taken advantage of the grace period and you're actually a month past due. If you have the statement date changed to the 12th, then add the number of days your issuer has for their grace period, (20 in this example) it now stretches past your end of the month pay. One call could save you hundreds of dollars just in adjusting your date by as little as a week.

Understanding Credit Card Interest

Picture a business with an unlimited supply of low cost product and a huge profit margin. That's the essence of a credit card operation. Plus they have millions of customers who carry a balance each month, many of whom choose to pay the minimum $60 to "avoid" the whole $2,000 bill. After all, a small $60 payment stalls off the balance for another month.

With three percent payments, very little actually goes to the principal. Of course, when consumers take advantage of the lower monthly payment, the interest costs keep increasing. Very bad for the holder, but very good for the issuer. To make matters worse, as of couple of years ago card issuers now increase your interest rate by five percent if two consecutive payments are made late, or three in one year. That brings the average card to over 24 percent. Another reason to assure that at least the minimum payment is made without fail, or the card is set up to automatically pay at least this amount through your bank.

At one point, the explanation of interest calculations was written in font maybe one-tenth of what you are reading here and was almost impossible to understand. Disclosure legislation has made reading and understanding them much easier. Yet the Financial Consumer Agency of Canada commissioned a study some years ago that found more than 40 percent of cardholders didn't know the interest rate of their own cards!

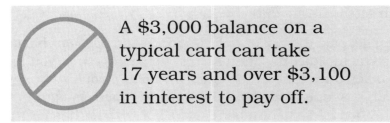

A $3,000 balance on a typical card can take 17 years and over $3,100 in interest to pay off.

Calculating All Those Interest Charges

Only a full payment of the balance avoids paying any interest. For everyone else, the following is an example of some transactions and ways interest is calculated. It assumes a 17 percent rate.

$ 75.00 charge	March 1	Balance: $ 75.00
$400.00 charge	March 8	Balance: $ 475.00
$250.00 charge	March 12	Balance: $ 725.00
$ 80.00 charge	March 15	Balance: $ 805.00

March 20 Statement balance	$805
Minimum payment due	$ 24
Grace period until	April 11
Payment made	$100 on April 11th

As the full balance wasn't paid, interest is charged on the full amount for the number of days as follows:

$ 75.00 Balance for 7 days (March 1-March 8)	= $ 0.21
$475.00 Balance for 4 days (March 8-March 12)	= $ 0.88
$725.00 Balance for 3 days (March 12-March 15)	= $ 0.99
$805.00 Balance for 27 days (March 15-April 11)	= $10.12
Total interest on April statement:	= $12.20

Old statement balance was	$805
Payment made	($100)
Interest is added for	$ 12.20
With no new charges, balance is now	$717.20

The interest free time is gone as you had until April 11th and didn't take advantage of it. So even paying the full $717.20 now means there will still be one more full month of interest. Once you haven't paid it in full, there is no free time ever on any charges until the balance is paid off and a new cycle starts. Their premise is to use it or lose it, and is now the case for almost all credit cards.

What Those Rates Really Mean

One of the best investments is always to pay off outstanding balances since the real cost of debt is significantly higher than most people realize. It is only with actual take-home (after tax) pay that credit card interest can be paid. Someone with $2,000 to invest might be happy with a return of seven percent, which is $140 a year. Since interest is taxable, even in the lowest tax bracket, this leaves a real return of $104.

How appealing would a totally risk free and guaranteed return of at least 24 percent be? Anyone with a credit card balance can have that opportunity. To calculate the real cost of interest, simply take one minus the marginal tax rate, then take the rate of the card and divide it by that figure. For example:

$1 - 0.30$ (tax bracket) $= 0.70$
Then a 19% credit card divided by this $0.70 = 27.1\%$ rate

At 19% credit card interest rate:	At 28.8% credit card rate:
In a 22% tax bracket 24.4%	36.9%
In a 30% tax bracket 27.1%	41.1%
In a 38% tax bracket 30.6%	46.5%

More than one dollar has to be earned to pay one dollar in debt after tax. It takes over $1,428 in earnings just to pay off a $1,000 balance for someone with a 30 percent tax rate. That makes the best credit card balance – no balance at all.

 Perhaps understanding this real cost should cause a little 'plastic surgery' ... cutting up some cards.

The Cheap Promotional Rate

From time-to-time certain issuers will mail out some very attractive rate offers. Most often they are zero, 1.9 or 2.9 per cent teaser rates. It's hard to do better, and as junk mail goes, it will certainly get a second look from many people.

Yes, a lower rate can translate into real savings, but only for a limited time. These offers vary, but generally have an attractive promotional rate for only six months, tops. It always pays to read the details closer than focusing on the big print. These rate promotions also tend to end immediately if the minimum payment is not made on time. After all, the card issuer is not trying to build delinquency – they want good clients that make their payments. During the promotional period, most will encourage you to transfer balances from other accounts without transaction fees, but only during this time. Remember that they want your balance way up there when the promotional period ends and the real rates start to apply.

If this is a new card application and you wish to switch your account, make sure to mark the end of the promotional rate on your calendar and have a firm and realistic game plan of how to pay the account off before that date. If you are transferring other accounts to this temporary low rate, remember they will only be transferred after you are approved and to the maximum of your credit limit. Do not assume your old bills are paid the day you are sending in your application but keep making payments until you know they are transferred.

 Promotional rates state in the fine print that they will immediately revert to full rate if any payment terms are not met.

What's The Best Card to Have?

Credit cards are not your friend and their convenience can quickly turn to a financial nightmare where the card and payments manage you, not the other way around. Everyone has different needs, wants and reasons to use their specific credit cards, however, the following are some valuable guidelines for different people:

Students: One credit card with a limit of $500 that you NEVER carry with you. The card is not for pizza and beer because the hangover of debt and interest can last for years.

If you regularly carry a balance: A low-rate 9.9% or 10.9% card. If it is from your own bank or credit union set up automatic payments so the minimum due is debited from account to protect your credit rating (you can still pay extra payments whenever you choose).

If you always pay off your balance: A card without an annual fee that allows you to collect the perks or points of your choice without indirectly paying for them through fees.

Couples: A different credit card for each partner. It assures you both have a credit rating and that you have one to use should your partners' card be lost or stolen on holidays.

For everyone who wants to get control of their spending: A "real" American Express card which is due in full each month. It assures you will never have a credit card balance again, which is a huge step towards financial freedom.

Congratulations! You're Pre-Selected

Credit card companies work with a huge database of existing clients. A larger customer base means volume, and volume means profit in merchant discount charges and annual fees. More accounts also mean a larger pool of cardholders that carry a monthly balance from which significant interest charges are collected as further revenue. But attracting new cardholders is always a challenge.

In North America almost seven billion, yes billion, pre-approved solicitations are mailed each year. Quite staggering, considering the response rate is less than 0.3 percent, yet that is still 21 million new accounts.

Almost all mailings these days are pre-selected instead. Even when the mailer shows pre-approved, the little asterisk will refer to a very hard to find spot that reads: "Subject to a credit bureau report and meeting income requirements." It also notes that you may not actually qualify at all. Getting a pre-selected application in the mail should only create as much excitement as that Publishers Clearing House letter stating you may have won already.

Killing Your Credit Card

Terminating a credit card is more than just putting it away, but that should definitely be the first step. The card is still perfectly valid and continues to stay active and alive. Obviously, the issuer will send out mailings to entice the holder to utilize the card again, as they want their card getting lots exercise – often.

To ensure a credit card is properly closed, the issuer must be notified. This can be done whether the card is paid in full or not. It is a simple matter of cutting the card in half. The next step is to mail a note asking for the account to be closed and the credit bureau advised. If there is still a balance, it only means the card cannot be used for new charges and does not affect the payments, which can still be paid like normal.

Chapter 4

Personal Loans:
The Inside Story

Consumer and personal loans come in all shapes, sizes and types. When money isn't borrowed on a line of credit or for a mortgage or vehicle, which are discussed in their own chapters, it's generally for consumer products. Personal loans aside, it is also the area where fees, gimmicks and promotions play a big part in convincing customers to just 'sign here' and have it today. What could be more convenient than finding the perfect stereo and a salesperson nearby that can get a credit application processed in less time than it takes to drive home and get the chequebook? Unfortunately, convenience does not often go hand-in-hand with the best financial terms. At worst, it's worth understanding what those offers really mean – and cost. But to start, some insight is needed into what goes on when lenders first see your application for any type of loan.

What happens behind the scenes after you apply for a loan is not really a mystery. Quite simply, the lender is checking out the odds of getting their money back if they say yes. The more money you want to borrow, the longer it will take, the more information you have to give them, and the more questions you will have to answer. It's really that simple.

A credit card application comes to a lender with thousands of others each day. It is a short application with a limited amount of questions which must be processed very quickly because of the volume. On the other extreme, applying for a mortgage involves a large number of steps. Sorry, nobody will lend you tens of thousands of dollars without a whole lot of questions, copies of your T4 and other hoops and questions.

Lenders do want to work with you to make an application into a loan. After all, they all have targets and goals to reach. They also have deadlines and other appointments, so stick to the subject and answer questions without window dressing, getting sidetracked, or sharing why your cousin couldn't fix your car before you get rid of it. For actual loans through a lender directly, supply factual information and bring along the backup you know they will need. Any delays are not their fault while you're hunting for paperwork. Lenders will not phone around for you, take your word on things, or be able to leave sections of their loan application blank – so be ready, do your homework and show up prepared and focused.

Be truthful and practice full disclosure with your loan officer. They will find out anyway whatever you try to hide, by accessing your credit bureau report. So you may as well avoid the embarrassment and get them on your side and wanting to work with you. Like people everywhere, lenders become very leery of helping you after you've spent the first part of the appointment bluffing, evading or wasting their time. That does not involve having to settle for partial answers, not having your questions explained thoroughly or being talked down to. After all, you are the consumer and you're the one who will ultimately be making them a lot of profit with the interest you will pay. You do have to do some negotiating as well. Lenders want to make a certain overall yield (profit) for their company. That does not mean they have to make it all from you, but they will start at their retail rates. In their perfect world, everyone pays this rate. But like the automotive business, how many people pay sticker price?

Every application for credit requires a signature before any credit checks are started due to consumer legislation in almost all provinces. It is your written consent for them to go ahead and check you out, to run your credit bureau report, and enter your application in their system.

The text above the signature is often as follows: "The undersigned warrants the accuracy and completeness of the above application and information. You are hereby authorizing us to obtain, verify and exchange credit and other information, including credit bureau reports from and with other persons with whom you have or propose to have financial dealings or where permitted or required by law." What this means is:

- You're signing to the accuracy and completeness of the application.

- You're agreeing that they can go ahead and do their credit checks with whomever they choose to contact. Consumer report means your credit bureau; employment verification is infrequently done, and the days of an actual call to your bank are long gone.

- You are giving the OK that they can keep exchanging information with other companies now and in the future.

For many personal loans, you will also need to decide whether you wish to have interest charged either on a fixed or floating rate basis. Both have their drawbacks and advantages.

Fixed rates have one consistent interest rate for the entire term of the borrowing. This is generally available if the term of the loan is five years or less.

Floating rates, also known as variable, are always adjusted. This change is covered by the loan agreement and is generally triggered at specific times. The amount of the change in interest is almost always in relation to the bank prime rate. That's the reason interest is often expressed in terms such as prime plus three. Because the rate will change with market conditions, it will generally be slightly lower. When rates are trending down, floating rate loans are a great idea, but in an environment where rates are moving upwards, it becomes a scary and risky scenario.

Finally, be careful when any retailer says: "We'll just do a quick credit application to get you pre-approved. It doesn't mean you're committed at all." Don't do it! A credit application should only be signed when you are ready to proceed to the next step – not when you're looking around. Your credit rating can be affected by a number of inquiries into your file. Being told a merchant needs this application to give you specific information is only sales pressure. Short of telling you whether you are approved or not, all other information can be obtained in advance without completing an application.

 Commit yourself to differentiating between shopping trips (looking) and spending trips (buying) and make them on separate days.

Can You Afford It?

If your income before taxes is $1,000 and you already have $500 in bills – sorry – you're not getting a loan of any kind, at any rate, from anyone, no matter how great the reason. The math says you can't pay it back and why would someone lend you money, when they know that you can't afford to make the payments in the future? All lending goes back to something called your debt ratio. They call it DSR, which is debt service ratio, or TDSR - total debt service ratio.

Your best intentions, excellent credit history or down payment will not make up for the fact that you do not have sufficient income on paper to qualify for the loan. There needs to be sufficient room in your gross pay to cover your current bills plus the new payment. Calculation sheets for this are at the end of the book, and it is something you can check before ever considering a loan application.

Your debt load ceiling cannot exceed 40 percent of gross income before tax. So it's a simple matter of taking your monthly pay times 0.4 to get the maximum amount a lender will allow towards payments. When your pay period is not the fifteenth and thirtieth, you will need to calculate your monthly income first:

- Every week – take your weekly gross pay times 52 divided by 12

- Every two weeks – take your bi-weekly gross pay times 26 divided by 12

If your pay includes bonuses or commissions that may not be on every pay period, it is best to take your total income over a six month period and divide it to get an accurate average per month.

From this 40 percent, you will need to subtract all your current payments. The chart for this is also at the end of the book. The expenses will include rent or mortgage, only the minimum payments on your credit cards (extra is great but not required), your current vehicle payments, personal loans and anything else. For example:

Gross income per month		$2,500
40% for debt load		$1,000
Current bills	Rent	$ 350
	Credit card payment	$ 45
	Furniture loan	$ 80
Total current bills		$ 475

$1,000 is the maximum debt load, and with $475 now owing it leaves $525 available for new borrowing. On the other end of the scale, if your current bills are already over $1,000, there is no chance of a further loan until some of these payments are out of the way. This calculation is the first thing your lender will do, so instead of being caught by surprise, it is an easy calculation to have the first hurdle cleared in wondering whether you will be approved.

With $1,000 available toward bills, there are a number of possibilities. There is $475 in bills already, so if the new loan has payments of that or less, you are within your maximum debt-load and the application can go ahead. Should the new loan have a $580 payment, you will not be approved, as it will push you over the maximum. But you could:

- Pay off your furniture loan, which would add $80 to your payment room.

- Use a down payment for your new loan to get the payments from $580 down to $525 or less.

- Add a cosigner whose income could make this possible (and only if that person has room on their debt load).

What's Your Net Worth?

Lenders all like to know what you're worth in total. Their question is, if everything goes badly, are the odds still good that they will get paid back? Is there enough money or assets to pay off all bills if everything were sold? On some applications, these questions are very limited. For larger loans or mortgages, there will be more that relate to your overall financial picture. In the back of the book is a calculation of your total assets – the things you own, and your total liabilities – the things you owe. It is a simple financial statement on yourself and gives lenders the big picture of what you're worth.

Even on simplified credit card applications, there will be a question asking if you are a homeowner or a renter. It tells them a number of things ranging from whether you have some equity (net value) in your home, to the mortgage payments that they use to calculate your debt-load. Often, even short-form applications ask for the house value and the mortgage amount for that same reason. Once again, the more you're borrowing, the more important this information becomes.

Collateral

All credit is extended on a secured or unsecured basis, which means it is with or without collateral for the loan. In the event collateral is given, the lender will hold a lien against the item until the loan is paid. Should you default on the payments, they will be able to seize or repossess the collateral you put up as guarantee for the loan. This collateral may or may not be enough to clear the balance if the payments are no longer made. It does, however give the lender a larger range of options should any default occur.

Generally, the larger the loan, the more likely it is the lender requires some security. A mortgage always has the house for security, while loans for a vehicle, RV or boat will almost always require the item being purchased for security.

Any loan without security is called a note, or signature loan. Unsecured credit is found with credit cards, overdrafts and many lines of credit. The better someone's credit rating, their stability at their job and residence, the less likely it is that amounts under five or ten thousand dollars will require collateral.

If They Say No

When you're declined for a loan the first thing to do is always to ask "why"? Not to storm out, get mad or defensive. You can't change or fix anything until you have some answers.

Were you declined because of insufficient income or total debt load? Well, both of these are areas where it is possible, and not that difficult to make changes. Are you applying for a loan that exceeds what you have for collateral – perhaps a lower amount will work? Would a cosigner be available to sign with you – could that be an acceptable alternative? It is always best to explore all your options instead of going from place to place expecting something different – their decision will likely be the same.

Perhaps you were declined because of a lack of stability. A red flag is always any frequent change of jobs. Yes, each position may be an increase in pay, or a better job, but their computers don't look at it that way and have no sympathy for the reasoning. Again, it is important to ask the right questions. In this case, how long will I need to be at my present employer to be reconsidered?

It could also be a result of previous credit problems. Lenders are not permitted to give you the specifics from your credit bureau report, but are only able to tell you that you were declined based on information in your file. Then you will need to get to work to find out the problem and verify the accuracy. Most people already know – just don't make the mistake of thinking every lender doesn't have access to that same information. You will not find any formal financial institution that skips the step of checking it. If bad credit is the issue, don't kid yourself into thinking you will talk them out of their decision. There are very few people with enough written documentation and backup proof to turn a declined loan into an approval – and only then with a significant down payment.

If You Can't Bank on the Banks

Always make your local credit union one of your stops when shopping for any financial needs or services. With more than five million members, almost 1,800 locations, and $105 billion in assets they are powerful competition to the typical no-service banks.

All of their financial services are competitive and their rates will often be lower. Where credit unions excel head and shoulders above banks is in their member service. Yes, you will be a member-owner and not just a customer. It might not sound like much, but you will quickly notice the difference. You will be doing business with a company that is very customer focused, where you are one of the owners and one that is based in your community. Credit unions also invest huge sums of money in their local communities through sponsorships of non-profit groups and charitable giving, as well as staff who volunteer year-round for many local projects.

Plus, at the end of the year you will actually receive a dividend back on your dealings with the credit union. Their profit sharing returns the vast majority of earnings back to members, since you are one of the owners! When was the last time your bank actually paid you?

Buy Now - Pay Later

To attract new business, many merchants frequently offer special deferred payment terms. The most common are 90 day no payment offers, no interest for any number of months or even a no payment, no interest, no down payment program.

All of these are still loans, they just have some twists designed to entice you to purchase now and avoid the pain of payments or interest – for a while. Even if payments, interest or both can be deferred, they still need to be paid eventually. But will that $1,000 sofa need to be replaced before it is even paid? At the very least, it will no longer look like it did new.

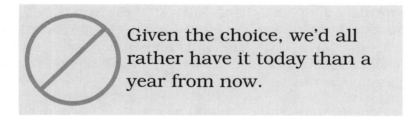

Given the choice, we'd all rather have it today than a year from now.

Careful thought should be given to whether delaying the inevitable start is really worth it. Frequently, consumers pretend or even believe that the debt is not real until the due date. The merchant certainly counts on that feeling when they market the program, but nothing could be further from the truth.

Merchants sell their finance contracts to outside lenders, most likely a finance company, for immediate cash. The well known Brick Warehouse, since becoming a public company has an in-house finance division. Future Shop and Best Buy deal with the giant GE Money for their retail financing, as does Wal Mart and a number of retailers.

In all cases, these arrangements allow the retailer to be paid immediately, when the financial institution buys the loan and actually collects the payments from the consumer. This will always be disclosed on the application, when it states just above the signature, the name of the actual lender.

Almost every company now charges an administration, documentation, processing, deferral, handling, or otherwise known fee. The fees are all the same, just called by different names and usually range from $39 to over $200. This charge is a profit for the merchant and used toward the costs of these offers. Since these types of financing promotions are hugely popular, we will look at each of them separately.

No Interest Promotions

This is a promotion that usually means an interest free period for six or sometimes 12 months. It requires monthly payments, but doesn't charge interest. If the loan is paid off during the term, it may be a fairly attractive proposition, but will involve paying a deferral or administration fee. Perhaps that still makes it worthwhile, or maybe the promotion is no longer that attractive.

To calculate your total price and payment, you will need to read the fine print of the advertisement or contact the merchant. What you need to know is the amount of the deferral charge and whether taxes and fees have to be paid up front, which is generally the case. On a $1,000 purchase for 12 months no interest (using five percent GST and seven percent PST in all examples) the breakdown would be:

Price	$1,000
Deferral fee	$ 60
GST & PST (or HST)	$ 127
Total amount	$1,187
Down payment (if any)	($ 187)
Balance financed	$1,000

You are financing $1,000, so your 12 payments will just be $1,000 divided by 12 for $83 per month, since there is no interest to add. You will also pay an additional charge of $60. If you take the fee divided by the amount financed times 100 you will see the actual cost of this loan: 60/1000 x 100 = An actual interest rate of 6 percent. Whether it is called a fee or interest, you're paying more than just the cost of the purchase. Plus you've paid taxes on this fee as well.

There is no such thing as free money. The merchant just absorbs the cost of interest. Sometimes the deferral fee covers it all, sometimes retailers cover the additional cost to get your business, or it is built into the price you are paying. When the contract is sold to the finance company, they will deduct the interest from the amount paid to the retailer. It will not be the full rate, but perhaps half the amount (wholesale to merchant) rate.

Remember: The fine print on the contract will tell you that if the balance is not paid in full by the date due, interest is charged right back to the first day of purchase. You snooze, you lose – that $1,000 interest-free will turn into owing $280 or more of interest one day after the due-date as the rates are generally 29% and that normally does not make the risk worthwhile.

It doesn't matter if it is called a fee or interest— it's still costing you money.

No Down Payments

Another component in these programs is often no down payment. This is the most perplexing element to understand for credit professionals. Every no down payment sale is always done OAC in the fine print, which is short for On Approved Credit. In most of these promotions, it also involves paying the applicable taxes up front. Perhaps a little misleading, but the amount they are willing to finance is only the purchase price, not the taxes. All financing without money up front will either increase the monthly payment or lengthen the time it takes to repay. For large ticket items, financing $10,000 instead of $8,000 at six percent, and skipping a $2,000 down payment means the:

- payment goes up by $61 (over 36 months) or $47 (over 48)

- interest increases by $186 (over 36 months) or $254 (over 48 months)

It's the old saying... you can pay it now, or pay it later. But later will always cost more—a lot more.

No Payments – For a While

Another offer is to promote a no payment plan. This is often used for larger ticket items where it can be of great appeal to many consumers. Obviously, payments will eventually need to be made and over a longer term because of the loan size. Is it an invaluable way to purchase something now and pay later or just the illusion of getting it today and for free – for a while?

 It's our continued optimism that next year will be better and we'll make more money to pay our growing debts.

For merchants it is an attractive advertising campaign used in the fall to defer the payments past Christmas. A 90-day deferral simply means that the first payment is not due for three months. The interest for this time is almost always included in the financed amount. Examples of this are detailed in the chapter on vehicle purchases, but are just as relevant for other consumer items.

Common Financing Arrangement

All retailers are in the business of selling their product lines. They're very good at what they do, and most of them operate in a competitive retail environment. Offering financing terms is another way to serve the needs and wants of their customers. Over the past number of years, advertisements based only on monthly payments have become more and more common. The largest reason is consumers' attraction to the monthly payments instead of the total price. It has also resulted in most sales staff often being the middlemen for lenders.

Retailers are not in the business of financing their products. They don't have hundreds of thousands of dollars to tie up in a credit department, nor do they want to hire dozens of staff to process applications and an equal number of collectors. Even huge firms like Sears have sold their credit operations to companies who specialize in this field, and have converted their accounts to a MasterCard through JP Morgan Chase Bank.

Retailers do want to make it convenient for consumers to buy their products. To accomplish this, they have set up arrangements with lenders to enable the sales staff to take credit applications, fax them to the lender and sign the paperwork right at the store. Each company makes their own decision of which lender they wish to work with. There are a number of ways to pay and any one of these is fine with the merchant.

- paying cash
- arranging your own loan
- increasing your overdraft
- setting up a line of credit
- purchasing on a credit card
- taking advantage of the merchant's credit offer

Here are a couple of examples of financing options and offers available through various national companies:

A well-known computer retailer with locations throughout Canada, assigns their finance contracts to Wells Fargo Financial. Their disclosure is simplified and easy to read but includes a notation that products are already cash discounted by three percent. So any purchase or down payment with a credit card will cost you an additional three percent fee.

Taking advantage of their financing also attracts an undisclosed administration charge ($99 for six months and $198 for 12 months when you call them) and some ads have shown a "Don't pay for 12 months" promotion. There is no mention of zero percent interest, which means you don't make the payments for a year, but the interest meter is running.

The actual finance contract discloses that it will be with Wells Fargo Financial at a rate of 28.9 percent. Their payment requirement is 1/36th (2.78%) of the unpaid balance or $25; whichever is greater each month. This is only $37 (on an example of $1,342 financed divided by 36) and takes over 86 months, or more than seven years, before the computer is paid off. Do you know many people happy with a seven-year old computer? Isn't that something to consider before paying minimum payments each month? Don't blame the merchant – nobody says a consumer has to choose those terms or that length of financing.

"Don't pay for 12 months" just makes this example even worse when considering the total amount paid back:

On a ficticious $1,000 computer:

Price	$1,000
Administration fee	$ 198
GST & PST (or HST)	$ 144
Total:	$1,342

Minimum payments result in $1,829 of interest. So it will be the $1,342 paid plus interest of $1,837 for a total of $3,179 (the $37 per month times 86 months). However it takes very little extra to pay it off within three years. This may better match the life of the payments to the (possible) life of the computer. It just means $56 payments, interest of $674, and a total paid of $2,016 (36 months x $56).

Frequently, one of the national department stores also advertises various finance options with either the "Do not pay for one year", or 12 equal payments - interest free. In both cases, a $65 deferral fee applies, the applicable rate is 28.8 percent and the purchase must be on their card. After all, what kind of marketing would it be if they didn't leave you with their credit card in your wallet to use over and over again in the future? A $700 furniture purchase offers a number of choices:

	Pay cash	12 months no interest	Don't pay for 1 year
Price	$700	$700	$700
Deferral fee	N/A	$65	$65
GST	$35	$38	$38
PST	$49	$54	$54
Down payment	N/A	($157)	($157)
Amount financed	nil	$700	$700
Payment/month	N/A	$58	0 for 1 year
Interest	N/A	none	$202
Total paid	**$784**	**$857**	**$1,059**

But: In the "Don't pay for one year" option, you have not paid for the furniture. You've just avoided the issue for 12 months. The $700 financed and $202 of interest for the year is now on your account and will require regular payments. If you take one more year to pay it off, you will have added another $147 in interest, or over two extra years almost $300. When all is said and done, the original $700 purchase will cost close to double. It is the reason these options never work in your favour. The risks of almost 30% interest and the guaranteed rip-off fees are never worthwhile.

The Fine Print of Advertisements

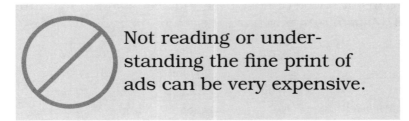

Not reading or understanding the fine print of ads can be very expensive.

The following is an example (yes, it's simplified here) of the text that you need to read carefully to understand the specific terms, fees and rates.

"Monthly interest is billed but will be waived if minimum monthly payments are made and the balance of the purchase is paid off by the end of the no interest period. Administration fee of $44.95 for 12 months contracts, when blended with interest will affect the annual percentage rate (APR). Example on 12 months no interest option: if minimum monthly payments totaling $611.14 on $1500 purchase are made and the balance is paid off within 12 months, interest is waived. Then the $44.95 administration fee creates an APR of 3 percent with total cost of $1,544.95 on $1,500 purchase. If you elect to finance for an additional 12 months and minimum monthly payments totaling $179.36 on $1,500 purchase are made and the remaining balance of $910.34 is paid off at the end of 24 months, interest charges calculated from the date of purchase plus administration fee are $634.65 (total cost $2,134.65) and APR is 26.91 percent for $1,500 purchase."

Simple right? You only need to imagine this disclosure in an ad roughly the same size print to fit on a postage stamp. What it actually means is:

- Purchase price of $1,500 with a $44.95 administration charge. If $611 in monthly payments is made for a year and the final balance is cleared, there is no interest to pay. Total pay back: The $1,500 purchase and $44.95 fee.

- Interest will be billed each month, but waived (not charged). They will bill it, but you won't have to pay it if you come through with a payment before the due date. One day, or more late, and interest at 26.91 percent is charged.

- To extend the contract beyond the 12 months attracts the same 26.91 percent rate, back to day one of the purchase. Take one day longer, you've lost the whole year of interest free.

- A term of 24 months at minimum payments still leaves a balance of $910. At this point, there will be $590 interest plus the $44.95 administration charge. If the $910 can then be found to pay this in full, the total amount would be $2,135. If not, the meter keeps running for a third year.

You need to make absolutely sure that:

- The balance owing can be paid in full the day it's due or interest starts at over 26 percent.

- The payment balance at the end of the one-year does not come from borrowed money or it will just be interest charges somewhere else.

- Pay the $1,500 plus $44.95 over 12 equal payments of $129 (i.e. ignore the minimum payment due) and be done with the contract in full at the end of the year. Spread the whole cost in your budget over a year or be ready for the pain of owing the balance and tons of interest.

- You decide if it is not wiser paying cash or making other arrangements. This avoids the delay of paying, as well as the chance of ever being a day late on a payment with interest this high. Plus it avoids the entire risk of these financing arrangements.

Are Lower Rates the Cheapest?

If it is only a question of rate, the answer is always yes. Unfortunately with fees and other charges, the answer is not always as simple as it seems. Which of these is better on a $2,000 loan for two years – nine percent with no fees, or six percent with a $95 fee? You can't just go by the rate alone and you always have to calculate the total you're paying back to find the answer. So looking up both from the loan charts in the back of the book shows:

$2000 @ 9% = $91/month x 24 months = $2,184 total paid

$2000 @ 6% = $89/month x 24 months = $2,136 + $95 fee = $2,231

(if the fee is financed as well, the interest is even higher)

It is important to see that only comparing rates is not a solution. You always need to look at the big picture, fees, charges and the TOTAL you are paying when it's all said and done. This includes anything you are paying for up front and all financing costs to get the actual total amount out of pocket.

Borrowing from Friends or Relatives

This is something beyond borrowing five dollars to go to the store because you forgot your wallet. For any larger amounts, if they don't lend you the money – you resent them. If they do – they resent you. Plus, if you don't pay promptly, you will likely avoid them as much as possible and won't really want to face them when you are not paying them back. They will also start judging whether and how you're spending your money. Christmas dinner will never taste the same again once you are in a loan with family members. Make it one of your last resorts and strictly a business deal.

- Put it in writing spelling out the amount, interest if any, and a specific repayment schedule. At the back of the book is a simple promissory note. It doesn't have to be complicated, it just has to be filled out and signed. Calculate the interest or a flat amount any way you agree, just make sure it is part of the payments. Why would your relatives or friends be any different than the bank? They won't lend you any money without something in writing either.

- Be honest in asking for what you need and how much.

- Be reasonable and real with yourself when deciding your repayments. Don't promise something you have no chance of meeting. Figure out what you can pay, just because there is no loan officer, it does not take the onus off you.

- Stick to your word – make the payments no matter what. Honour them by paying on time, as they trusted you with the loan – when (perhaps) others turned you down.

Don't Forget!

- There is no such thing as a stupid question – it's YOUR money. If you're uninformed it will cost you.

- Don't assume – ask!

- When in doubt – get it in writing in a way that makes sense to you – don't just let them point to a clause in the contract that even a law professor would have to think about.

- Get the fees, additional charges and totals fully outlined.

- The merchant is disclosing what they are (hopefully) required to – on their terms – in their language – in their best light. Stop them when they use jargon or when you have questions.

- Salespeople are not credit managers. They may be very good at product knowledge but they won't (and shouldn't) give you any financial advice. Knowing the questions to ask and getting the right answers is entirely up to you.

- At the end of the day, it is YOU that makes the loan payments – so the time to think it through and ask questions before signing.

 If your banker sounds like a salesman, professor or politician, consider going somewhere else.

Chapter 5

Automobile Loans

Be careful reading this whole chapter at once, as you will likely just get a headache. To paraphrase consumer advocate Phil Edmonston: There's the truth, there's fiction and then there's automobile-speak.

 There is no such thing as too much information and homework when it comes to automobile shopping.

Long gone are the days when everyone could afford to trade in a vehicle every two or three years. Pressure on the manufacturers and lost sales to imports have vastly improved the quality and warranty of almost all vehicles. This makes it possible for consumers to keep their vehicles for a longer period of time – either by necessity or choice. They are also more expensive – which means less chance that anyone can afford to just write a cheque.

Plus, anyone trying to save enough to pay cash sees that the goal posts keep moving. Average new vehicle prices have increased at far greater rates than inflation. It is not because car manufacturers are greedy or less productive than other businesses. A large part of their costs are the ever-evolving technological advances that most consumers demand. Years ago it was the delay wiper, now a standard feature, but that was a far smaller cost than airbags, ABS breaks, Global Positioning Systems, backup sensors and even more expensive technology just around the corner.

The sections in this chapter are broken down into the most common areas of finance or leasing, as well as the various options, rebates, rates, and other choices. The same information also applies to boats, skidoos and recreation vehicles. Their purchases may not be as common, but these industries operate very much like the automotive business.

From the original times of financing the first Model T cars, the area of automobile, boat and RV financing has come a long way. When anyone spends this much money, a lot of research, consideration and thought goes into the purchase. Unfortunately, how to pay for it often becomes an after-thought. But just like shopping for a house and mortgage, this is an area that is even more important than finding the vehicle itself. So before immediately racing to the bank to simply sign the first loan agreement offered, it is always a good idea to at least speak to the dealership finance department. The main reason is that many manufacturers often have very attractive terms and rates that they directly subsidize. That makes them real deals, instead of those which are hidden in the price of the purchase, and will be available only through the dealer. If nothing else, it will give you a great head start on your financial shopping if you can trust yourself to fight the urge to get it all done on the spot without exploring your options.

It is the responsibility of the business office to ensure the financing happens and terms are acceptable to the purchaser. Make no mistake, it is a large profit centre, and the business manager is on commission. But in some dealerships they can actually be financial experts that know their way around the world of credit. Without getting your financing looked after one way or another, there would not be a sale. Unfortunately many are ex-salespeople that train themselves on the job and are often not equipped or experienced to offer much credible financial advice beyond the basics.

Don't worry, there is no need for a financing course. You just need to understand that there are three main factors influencing any loan. These are the interest rate, the term and the total amount borrowed. Oh, and then there are the gimmicks, free trips and limited time offers. All of them ending with that famous phrase: "see dealer for details."

The ideal financing for your vehicle should be set up within your budget and on your terms with the main goal of making the payments end as quickly as possible. It should be a fixed payment schedule where there is a definite end in sight. Plus it should NEVER have you owing more on the vehicle than it's worth and the financing should NEVER be longer than its useful life. Yet unfortunately this happens thousands of times a day all across the country with painful and expensive consequences. Sometimes this means just being honest in realizing you really can't afford the vehicle you have your heart set on.

Some of the most dangerous situations that create problems, extra expense and no hope of trading in the vehicle early are:

- small or no down payments
- financing the taxes
- taking the longest term available
- vehicle shopping on payments alone
- buying a vehicle beyond a set budget of price or payments
- taking advantage of special offers without realizing the costs and implications
- longer term financing on used vehicles which is beyond the reasonable life-expectancy
- trading a vehicle and adding its balance to the new one for more than the trade-in was worth
- signing a lease without understanding the mileage or tax implications
- not comparing the choice of rebates vs. rate breaks in total pay back costs
- trading in after two or three years while financing for five
- pretending to pay cash by adding it to a mortgage or line of credit hoping to make lower payments

This last point deserves a special mention as it happens quite frequently. Customers are re-mortgaging or adding a second mortgage, to pay cash for their purchase as they see it. Nothing could be further from the truth. If this new mortgage is amortized over five or six years, it may make sense. Unfortunately that is hardly ever the case. Mortgages are set up for very long terms and now include money to pay for the vehicle. This creates the dual challenges of having payments hidden in the mortgage for much longer than the life (or ownership) of the vehicle and potentially costing significantly more in interest.

A ten- or twenty-year mortgage for a five- or seven-year vehicle life is never a good idea.

Throughout this chapter we will use a fictitious car as a comparison. Each example uses the five percent GST and seven percent PST (or HST total) for ease of comparison. If your tax is higher, it will only have a small impact on the examples. Conversely, if you live in Alberta without PST, the comparisons are still valid, your totals will just be slightly less.

The fictitious 2009 Coolcar has a price of $25,760 after all the taxes are included. To add this amount into a mortgage does reduce the payments, but costs way more interest and over a longer period of time.

Financed	Term	Payment	Total interest paid
Car loan	4 year	$611	$ 3,565
at 6.5%	5 year	$504	$ 4,484
	6 year	$433	$ 5,420
Mortgage	10 year	$273	$ 6,950
at 5%	15 year	$203	$10,784

Let's face it, financing is a necessity for any large ticket items for most people. On the surface, who wants to spend $20,000 when you can spend only $395 for the same vehicle (per month)? Hence the main force behind advertisements is now geared more towards promoting payments and not the price. In fact many ads now show a lower price while noting in the fine print "based on $2,000 down-payment" just to soften the blow. It makes reading car ads meaningless without also reading the fine print and the details of the financing disclosure. When you are financing the vehicle you will need to make a decision before ever leaving the house. Do I just want to worry about the monthly payment today or the big picture of the total you have to pay? It will matter a lot in the future.

Buy New or Used?

Ah, there is nothing quite like that new car smell is there? Never been driven, no dings, has all the latest options, full warranty and your choice of colour. All your friends will also know that you stepped up to the plate and went first class. Besides, it's something most people only get to do two or three times in their life. Plus manufacturers offer a rebate or subsidized interest rate almost year round in an effort to earn your business. Let's face it, the manufacturers have no vested interest in selling a used vehicle. It has been sold once already, they've made their money – only new vehicles keep the factory running and pay their bills. Yes, dealers sell used vehicles, but rebates and their great rates will always be restricted to marketing their brand new models.

For dealers, it's a competitive world too. The days of big markups are mostly gone and they're often lucky to make single digit returns on a sale of base new models. Whether they like it or not, it is a volume game for dealers, just as much as the manufacturer. In those cases the new vehicle salesperson you are buying from might make enough commission to pay half your first payment at best. Consumers have become much more educated, and ask lots of questions, which often translates to minimum wage by the time the sale is done.

For all the positives, when you purchase a new vehicle, it is important to understand that you are not buying an asset. Your vehicle will not be worth more next month than it is on the dealer's lot. The depreciation is different for every model. But an easy way to find out is to check the price of a comparable one-year old model through ads or on the dealers' used car lot. A general guide is around 20-30 percent the first year, and 60 percent for the first four years.

Then there is the issue of taxes. The more you pay, the higher your taxes will be since they are based on the purchase price. With a trade, the GST will be on the difference you are paying, as is the case for PST in most provinces. But still, paying more for the vehicle also means paying more tax.

When purchasing a used vehicle, it will definitely take a little more work. You also have to be flexible and a little sharper when it comes to the price. After all, no two are exactly alike, which makes comparison shopping more challenging. One has low mileage; while the other has more features – one has new tires while another...and so on.

You also will not get a cool rate or rebate, but you will definitely pay less than the price of a new one. On used vehicles, promotions such as rebates, trips or toasters are covered by the seller and are built into the price. It might still be a good deal, but anything added to the cost will naturally drive the price up – there is no such thing as free anything. It is also unlikely that the seller will just absorb the price of these gimmicks since they also have to make money on the deal.

You will also avoid the GST if you are purchasing a used vehicle privately. Through a dealer you will still pay taxes; it will just be on a less expensive vehicle. There are no right or wrong answers – many consumers are just more comfortable with a reputable dealer instead of a private seller. It is only an issue of your budget and the affordability of payments. In fact, there is a large group of consumers who strictly view vehicles as basic transportation that just needs to be reliable and have a warranty. This group is drawn to the one-year old lease returns, which were actually short-term rental cars for around six to 12 months.

If you have decided on a new vehicle, you will need a bit of a road map to guide your way through the minefield of offers. The vast majority of problems occur when customers arrive at the dealership expecting one thing and finding out something quite different. For most, shopping starts with a look through the newspaper ads or some offer on the radio. Manufacturers advertise as well – quite a bit in fact. But their ads are generally targeted to a national audience and promote specific models, their features and values and their ads will have the best disclosure information. But the real competition for your business is on the ground between dealers.

 The average new vehicle purchaser keeps his or her vehicle more than seven years.

Take the Rebate or Cool Rate?

One of the first decisions you will have to make when you've found your new vehicle is whether you want the factory subsidized rate or a cash rebate. With very few exceptions, they are always offered as an either-or. Great rate breaks target the majority of customers who make their decision based on payment terms. For this very budget sensitive group, a change of $20 or $30 might well send them to the competition in search of a lower payment. In order to keep attracting cash purchasers as well, the manufacturers offer a rebate. There are times, however when the cool rate is actual zero. When that is the option, even cash customers think twice about their choice.

The main point to understand for rebates is that they are taxable. Governments treat rebates as essentially a factory down payment. The rebate is deducted from the amount you owe and not the price you pay. To get the net amount, take the rebate divided by the taxes to get the net (real) amount. So a rebate of $3,000 divided by 1.12 for taxes is actually $2,679.

Ads are always quoted AFTER the rebate is deducted. No dealer wants to advertise a higher price than necessary. So every ad assumes the customer is paying cash and not financing. Yet in that same ad, when you see the payments advertised, they use the cool rate instead. It is very misleading, but a dealer does not want to advertise a higher payment than necessary. All the fine print (hurray for disclosure legislation) shows rebates and rate programs are mutually exclusive. It means one or the other, but not both. The ad will also show that the price is 'rebate to dealer.' That's where the rebate has already been deducted to come up with the price you are seeing. OK, do you have a headache already? It is not that difficult to understand with an example.

This is our fictitious 2009 Coolcar again with an advertised price of $20,000 and the fine print showing: with rebate to dealer. What this means is that the price is really $23,000, then it's your choice of 2.9 percent financing or a $3,000 rebate. What they are saying is: We have advertised it using the rebate so we can show the lower price to get your attention. We know more than three-quarters of you will finance, but we will deal with adding the rebate back in when you arrive.

The full information actually breaks down as follows:

Price	$23,000
GST	$ 1,150
PST/HST	$ 1,610
Sub total without rebate	$25,760
Less the rebate	($ 3,000)
Total amount you owe for the car	$22,760

If you are paying cash, that's the amount unless the dealer charges other fees or you purchase anything additional.

Finance choice #1: Take the cool 2.9 percent rate from the manufacturer for a four-year term. Down payments are always important, but in these examples they have been omitted. Total amount for the financing is $25,760.

At 2.9 percent over 48 months, payments will be $569 per month and you are paying back a total of $27,312 (48 x $569). A total of only $1,552 interest, but then you gave up the rebate.

What almost all customers miss is that there is another option. What if you would like to use the rebate, because it's a large amount and comes straight off the total price right now? Using the rebate means you are financing a lot less, but then cannot get the advertised rate. However you can take regular bank rates and still keep your cash rebate. A great rate helps a little bit each month while a lump sum rebate comes off the top immediately to finance a lot less. The price of the vehicle is still $25,760 less the rebate for a total of $22,760. At 6.5 percent, the payment is $540 for four years. Hopefully you have already noticed that this is $29 less than using the 2.9 percent rate! The total amount you are paying is $540 times 48 months or $25,920. Yes - $1,392 less, even though your interest rate is higher. If you are having flashbacks to your last purchase, this will serve as a reminder that there are always options available if you take the time to ask questions and do the math.

Always add up the full amount of down payment and monthly charges to calculate your real costs with all three possibilities.

Down Payments

The less you finance the better and the sooner the debt is paid off. So, when it comes to down payments, more is always better. It will save interest and reduce the monthly payments. Our example has $2,760 in taxes, and without a down payment to at least take care of this amount, it adds $382 in interest and increases the payments by $65 per month over four years just to cover taxes.

When the sale is made, the dealer remits all taxes to the governments, whether the sale was cash (dealer has it collected) or financed (they are part of the loan). Yet without a down payment, their hangover becomes part of the payments and debt for the entire life of the loan.

Without paying at least the taxes up front, significant challenges can arise later. Should you sell or write off the vehicle in a year, you have paid less than $800 out of $2,760 in taxes owing and financed. Since they are in each payment over the full term, you still have most of it as part of the loan. After only one year there is still a large amount owing on the vehicle and another $2,000 in taxes as part of it.

Zero Percent Financing

Finally something that is easy to understand. This is a promotion many manufacturers have run from time-to-time. It is very expensive because they are subsidizing the entire interest cost, therefore it can often be something close, like a 0.9 percent rate. It is an offer that even cash buyers frequently take advantage of since their savings can stay in the bank and keep making (taxable) interest of some kind.

To calculate the monthly payments, simply take just the total financed divided by the term of the loan. For our example it is $25,760 divided by 48 months, which makes the payments $537. The total pay back is the same as the amount financed, since there is no interest to calculate.

When this promotion comes from a used car department, someone has to pay the interest charges. These are generally promotions with offers of three or six months meant to attract additional business. The fine print will show that the maximum term is at most 12 or 24 months on selected vehicles and varies by year or model. The cheaper the vehicle, the less costly the promotion for the dealer who is, after all, writing a cheque to the lender for the actual cost of interest. Is this cost included in the price?

Any comparison-shopping will quickly discover the answer. If so, what's the point of overpaying for the vehicle just to receive some benefit back on the financing?

Do Not Pay Until 2015

OK, maybe not quite that long, but dealerships do advertise no payments for three, four or even six months. Is that good news or a bad idea? From a marketing perspective it is certainly a very good promotion. It works – so they keep doing it – in many more industries than just automotive. It draws customers for one reason or another that would otherwise not be considering their purchase – at least, not yet. But you have to be realistic. If you really need the no payment period what will be different by that time? Will you really have an after-tax raise to make the payments? Not likely. Will another bill be completely paid off so that you can take that amount and use it for the vehicle payment? Or are you just wanting the vehicle today and delaying the inevitable payments?

This promotion is called a payment deferral. But it is not a guaranteed offer for everyone. The advertisements always state OAC: On Approved Credit. Deferral terms are given only to those applicants with above average credit and without maximum debt loads. Yet these are the clients that find the promotion most attractive. For lenders, it's a higher risk since they know that payments might not start for six months and the vehicle is still depreciating. The lender won't be getting money from you, or even hear from you, for some time to come. Yes, many customers love the no payment option and often view this as a temporary free car. Nothing could be further from the truth.

The two most important factors to keep in mind are that:

- The interest meter is running – it does not state interest free.

Three, four or six months are still accumulating while you are not paying it or anything towards the principal.

- The value of your vehicle is decreasing during this time while your loan is increasing.

Back to our fictitious (this time used) Coolcar using six months no payments:

Price of vehicle	$23,000
GST & PST (or HST)	$ 2,760
Less down payment	($ 3,000)
Total financed	$22,760

Since these are generally used vehicles, we will keep using the 6.5 per cent bank rate. On a five-year loan, you will still have 60 payments; they just won't start for six months. So you really owe the money for five and a half years instead.

The payments will be 60 x $460, which has blended in (included) the interest during the six months of no payments. That amounts to $123 for each month – a total of $740. Your total pay back will be 60 x $460 or a total of $27,600.

You've financed $22,760, but at the end of the first six months you haven't even started. Yet on that date, your balance is really $740 higher and you now owe almost $24,000. Six months into the start of your payments – a year from the purchase date – and your balance will still be $21,500.

All Those Other Gimmicks

Many people believe you can tell a lot about the professionalism and credibility of a dealership by their promotions. Whether that's accurate or not, some of the more questionable ads must be working or they wouldn't keep using them. Often these do cross the line, or come very close, to breaching provincial consumer legislation. When they involve spending your hard-earned money or financing, it's worth a quick review:

Buy at Invoice – Priced at Dealer Cost – Zero Direct Profit Sales

No, not quite, sorry. Dealers are in business to make money. There is no shame in that, since it allows them to employ hundreds of thousands of people across the country and many dealers are great corporate citizens in their community. However there are some that want you to believe they will never ever make a profit – at least not from your purchase. For these promotions, always have a look at the fine print. If it is missing, be very careful of a dealership that does not fully disclose detailed specifics. The first thing to note is that rebates and incentives are assigned to the dealer. When all the rebates are signed over to them, it can make some of these offers possible. There are also manufacturers who have sales incentives included in the factory invoice, which is passed to the dealer after the sale. So it might say zero direct profit but it doesn't say zero profit. Once again – buyer beware.

Just because you're sitting on the other side of the desk doesn't mean you're not in control.

Lenders on Site to Fight for your Credit Approval

No, sorry again. The lenders are at home on the weekends and after 6 p.m. when you're likely to go vehicle shopping. The dealer has the paperwork from many lenders, so they can take the applications on their behalf. But they are not in the back office with a coffee just waiting to wrestle over your deal and auction off the lowest rate. Besides, it's a competitive environment for them as well. Any small rate change by one quickly has others matching it to keep their share of business.

Double your Down-Payment

Well, sort of. This type of ad always discloses that it is up to a maximum of $750 or perhaps $1,000 total. So they are contributing half that amount but often already advertise their used vehicle prices with this amount deducted. So the advertised amount is often not the real figure. Is it a deal or just included in the price? Only a little comparison-shopping will answer that question for sure.

Absolute Lowest Payments

Yes, they may be. But the lowest payment is always the absolute longest time financed. Once again it is important to look at the disclosure. They may be using seven-year payments. It could be the lowest, but is that the primary factor? You will see the text of: Payments based on 60 months, amortized over 84 months at x percent.

That makes it a 60 month rate, which will then get adjusted, since the whole loan is calculated over 84 months or seven years. It is another example where $20 or so might take a full year or two off the finance term.

It is not the dealership's job to talk you out of things— that is totally up to you.

We Accept all Credit Applications with Guaranteed Approval*

Sad but true that it is estimated over 20 percent of the population are unable to qualify for conventional loans due to credit problems, bankruptcy or many other reasons. The financing hope for this group is generally termed subprime financing. It comes with rates up to 29 percent and huge fees, if there is an approval at all. While it is a very profitable area for dealers, it does involve vast amounts of work and challenges with a below average approval rate. Advice to these clients can fill an entire book on its own. Unfortunately, these ads do very little but encourage consumers falsely. Again, it is the job of the advertisement to get you in the door – in this case to give hope and encouragement.

As the tiny asterisk in the heading shows, the fine print will include words to the effect that down payments may be required for guaranteed approval. Interest rates may vary from zero to 29 percent. Where on the credit risk scale would these people be? Certainly not anywhere near the zero percent side of the equation. Yes, every application is accepted – that just means holding their hand out and saying thanks for giving us the credit application – it has nothing to do with being accepted. After all, anyone can have an approval, a worse case scenario is a 95 percent down payment, isn't it?

Only a few lenders deal with credit challenged applications and every dealer is sending them to these same ones. If nothing else, anyone who falls into this category needs to understand that applications at more than one or two dealers will result in the same answer as the application is ending up at the same lenders on the other end of the fax machine. Sadly, however the need for transportation has thousands of Canadians making finance payments where the interest is more than the original price of the vehicle.

We Make Half Your Payments

Until when? This promotion allows dealers to advertise monthly payments of half the real amount. Then the fine print discloses this payment is applicable for only four or six months before it reverts to the real amount. The finance contract has to be obtained through the dealer and are usually not at their best available rates. After all, they do need to make a larger referral fee from the lender to subsidize this promotion. Plus the contract will always be for the absolute longest term so their half of some payments is the smallest amount.

Extra Fees and Charges May Apply

Well yes, they will apply and the list can be lengthy. One of the most expensive is often the added charge for delivery. Most North American Manufacturers include them in the vehicle pricing. Imports often do not – but dealers are free to determine the amount. If they are selling the vehicle in your town, shouldn't they pay to get it there? A few calls on this quote may save you even more money than shopping around for the interest rate.

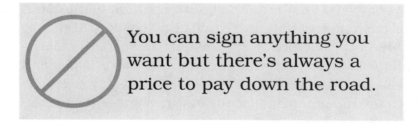

You can sign anything you want but there's always a price to pay down the road.

When Something Has Gone Wrong

Last but not least, all these contracts are covered by something called the doctrine of holder-in-due course. This legal wording simply means the company doing the financing is protected. The lender purchased the contract in good faith and payments have to be made. No matter what dispute the buyer has, from misrepresentation to faulty merchandise, or a host of other problems, the issue is not with the lender. They were not involved and have a right to be repaid. The buyer can certainly pursue the seller through whatever means available, but cannot withhold payments to the lender.

Balloon Financing

Balloon contracts have been around for some time, but have only come to prominence in the last few years. They were a response by some banks to the option of leasing. Banks are not directly allowed into the leasing business under the current Bank Act. It is an area they would dearly love to compete with vehicle manufacturers, but will have to await the next round of reviews by the Federal Government. Since leases often produce lower monthly payments, this allows the banks an option to offer clients similar results using a different method.

The major difference from leasing is that balloon loans require all taxes to be included up front. They are three, four or five year loans with this balloon amount owing at the end. After the completion of the actual finance portion of the contract, the customer is able to return the vehicle without being liable for the balance owing. Just like leases, this creates the option of walking away if the amount left owing is higher than the value of the vehicle. Pay only about half, pay only what you use and other similar slogans are some of the marketing phrases used.

Different lenders have different rules, but you will always be liable for any over-mileage on the vehicle and damage beyond normal wear and tear. Most of them also have a drop-off or termination charge ranging from $200 to $400 for the right to walk away. In the event that the balloon balance is worth paying, it will still mean re-financing that amount at prevailing rates if you are not able to pay cash for the balance due. Don't be surprised, however if it turns out that after all those years of payments, the balloon amount is almost the same as the vehicle is worth. The end-value calculation comes from a guide published by the same people that create the famous Black Book of used car values. These guides just project future values four or five years ahead. They are not designed to help build equity, they are only meant to have the payments close to break even with the balance owing versus the value at the end.

Where to Finance

When the time comes to deal with the financing, there are three main avenues. It should never be an issue of finding the fastest, but rather the one with the best financial terms available. When you have found your perfect vehicle, a small deposit will always hold it, which is fully refundable, if it is clearly marked as deposit subject to suitable financing.

Financial institutions get their automotive business either directly from customers walking into the branch or indirectly by having them referred from the dealerships. Direct lending lets them market to their own clients, do their own applications, sell their own products and complete all the paperwork. They will take the serial number of the vehicle used for collateral, process the loan and issue a bank draft to pay for the purchase.

Indirect lending is financing through the dealership. Lenders still have control over the credit decision, but do all their processing in one office behind the scenes. In return, they pay dealers a referral fee, generally a flat amount of the total loan depending on the rate charged. Credit applications are faxed to the lenders' automotive division and a response comes usually within three or four hours. The contracts are then signed with the dealer outlining the full details of the loan and pledging the vehicle as collateral. After that, the contract is sold to the lender to whom all payments are actually made.

This arrangement sometimes allows dealers to use their volume to an advantage. It won't make a bad application into a good deal, but occasionally will make it possible to get an approval for a marginal client. After all, for anyone with questionable credit, it is nice to have someone with a vested interest fighting on your behalf. If there is no approval there won't be a sale either.

The third source is the finance division of the manufacturer. Some of the better known are General Motors Acceptance (GMAC), Ford Credit Canada, Chrysler Credit Canada and Honda Canada Finance to name a few. All new vehicle low rate financing goes through them, depending on which manufacturer.

So a low rate finance contract on a new Nissan will need to be done through a Nissan dealer and can only be financed with Nissan Motor Acceptance.

In good times or bad, the larger operations like Ford Credit contribute literally billions of dollars to the bottom line of their parent companies. Their mandate is to make a profit, but also to serve their dealers. In Canada, Ford Credit can approve an application in less than a minute, if it falls within certain criteria. The business manager simply enters the application onto a computer screen and presses the send button. On a large percentage, an approval will flash across their screen in an instant. The application is scored; a credit bureau report pulled and the figures on the vehicle purchase are reviewed. Yes, it impresses customers, but then the name of the game is to get the customer from purchase decision to delivery in as little time as possible. GMAC's equivalent system optically scans faxes in a centralized system that can also grant approvals in mere minutes based on your credit score. The rest of the applications are forwarded to a regional office where they are reviewed individually. In other words, the system can approve, but it always takes a real person to decline an application.

Leasing Made Simple

A lease is an alternate way of paying for a part of your vehicle. It is the automotive equivalent of "Pay as you go" cell phones. To reduce payments, a lease takes the future value of the vehicle out of the amount financed. It allows payment for what you are using and not the entire vehicle. That part left out of the financing for the end is called the residual or buyout. So on a three-year lease, the estimate might be that the vehicle is worth 40 percent at the end. On $20,000, that takes $8,000 off and charges principal payments only on the other $12,000. There will still be interest on the whole amount – after all you're driving the whole vehicle, but you are paying back only the $12,000 that you are using.

But: when the three years are over, the vehicle isn't paid for. The $8,000 that was left out now has to be dealt with. It is entirely your option of what to do and your choices at the end of the lease are to:

- Walk away from the buyout balance – after all if it's not worth that much, why would you want to pay it? Dropping off the vehicle does mean you will have nothing to drive and nothing to show for years of payments. Plus the company will charge you for any damage, missing equipment and extra kilometers since every lease comes with a restricted amount or there will be a bill for the extra driving.

- Sell it or trade it – you still owe $8,000 plus the taxes but anything more than that is yours (it is called the equity – the difference between what you owe and what it's worth).

- Re-finance the balance to finish paying it off. It takes the $8,000, adds taxes and finances it for another term.

 If you choose to lease: Longer terms reduce the financial advantage. A lease longer than three years seldom makes sense.

You can negotiate the price on a lease the same way as a purchase. It will affect your payment. The buyout at the end doesn't change – it is always set based on a percentage of the sticker price so it is the same for everyone. However, a lease is not like renting a car for a couple of months. You cannot simply return the vehicle at your convenience before the end of the contract. It is called an early termination and will be expensive.

Leasing has been an alternate method of financing for decades. Until the late 1980's, it was mostly restricted to businesses with consumer leasing less than four percent of the total. That all changed rapidly in the 1990's. The finance arm of General Motors, GMAC, in some years processed in excess of 100,000 contracts. Leasing reached its peak in 1997 with almost half of all new vehicle sales, but has backed off significantly since then.

Ford has always been seen as the leader in leasing. They were the first to recognize that customers can have a reasonable payment for a short term, and dealers were able to have a ready made supply of good, late-model used vehicles when customers traded in their leases. After all, a $2,000 down payment over only 30 months means a drop in payments of $67. That identical $2,000 when used on a 60-month contract only impacts the principal for $33 per month. When a customer has that amount in their hand, it always seems better to cut $67 off the payment than $33.

The tremendous explosion of leasing quickly became a challenge for manufacturers. The biggest problem was the vast number of lease returns. The original goal was to get people to trade their vehicles more rapidly and still applies to large numbers of customers. Unfortunately, they had to find a home for the huge number of the returned vehicles. That became expensive and flooded the market with some manufacturers having upwards of five or ten thousand vehicles dropped off in a particular month.

As a result, their attractiveness has been scaled back with industry reports showing manufacturers losing literally hundreds of millions of dollars on end-value guarantees that proved to be too optimistic. Terms have now been stretched to keep the vehicle on the road a little longer, while the super-attractive rates have been scaled back to make leases more viable for manufacturers, but less so for consumer. Residual (end) values have also become more conservative to work with a more realistic (lower) end value designed to reduce the number of consumers just dropping off their vehicles.

Experts estimate that leasing is a good choice for around one-third of new vehicle buyers.

Is leasing an attractive alternate to financing? For a few people, certainly. Is leasing an advantage over financing – maybe. Each vehicle is as different as the needs of a customer. Not every client (hopefully) only considers the payments. It is also an issue of the total pay back and, in the case of leasing, other factors as well.

Back to our 2009 Coolcar, either on a lease or purchase. This example is based on no down payment, using both the GST and seven percent PST for simplicity and ignores all other taxes, levies, kinky or questionable fees and charges.

	Purchase	Lease
Manufacturer Sticker price		$24,700
Price of vehicle	$23,000	$23,000
Taxes	$ 2,760	$ nil
Total starting balance	$25,760	$23,000
Rate	6.5%	3.9%
Term	60 months	48 months
Base payment		$ 342
Tax on payment	N/A	$ 41
Total payment	$ 504	$ 383
Buyout balance (37%)	nil	$ 9,139
Tax on buyout	N/A	$ 1,097
Total pay back	$30,240	$28,620

Explaining the lease:

- A lease is paying for a portion of the vehicle, and only deals with the buyout balance at the end.

- Tax with leases is paid on each monthly payment. Yes, this means tax is also on the interest part of the payment, so the taxes will be more. It will also be charged on the buyout balance if the vehicle is purchased at the end of the term.

- If the customer wishes to keep the leased vehicle at the end, the balance will be $9,139 and the other $1,097 in taxes. Or, a new loan will be set up to finance this for another two years ($708 interest) or three years with $1,059 interest.

- Lease payments show the base payment only and the taxes are added later. Once again, the intent is to advertise the lowest amount possible.

- You will be charged your first payment and a refundable security deposit that will be held for the term of the lease, similar to renting an apartment.

- There are always kilometer restrictions on the vehicle. The ads usually include 20,000 km of driving per year. Higher usage makes the vehicle worth less over time. This can result in significant penalties over the limit if the vehicle is returned. Any lease can be structured to meet actual needs with a corresponding lower buyout.

If a low payment is the only consideration, a lease will often be the answer. The end buyout is a percentage of the sticker price. It is not calculated off the negotiated price, but is always the same figure. Price always impacts the payment; but the buyout is a fixed percentage set by the manufacturer. This is the area where they have direct control over the volume of leases by managing the payments. If they choose to increase the percentage of the buyout, it will leave less to pay each month and result in a higher balance at the end. Moving this percentage up by nine percent means the payments will drop by $48 but the buyout at the end will jump by $2,223. This would now allow the payment to be $299 and brings this Coolcar under $300 for an advertisement.

Some basic leasing advantages:

- you are not financing your taxes up front
- down payment has a bigger impact on payments
- monthly payments are generally lower
- terms are almost always (or should be) shorter
- someone else has the risk of guessing the future value and the problem of getting rid of it if they guessed wrong on the valuation
- no pretending it is an asset to pay off as quickly as possible. It is just an expense each month like cable TV
- maybe you can only afford a Focus, but leasing might let you drive a Mustang

Some disadvantages of leasing:

- the interest charges are for the full amount of the vehicle price, but the principal payments are only on the price less the end-value (the reason for lower payments)
- you are responsible for mileage and excessive wear & tear
- two or three years from now, the balance owing will still be approximately what it's worth – there will not be much, if any, equity
- if you're keeping it, there will be another round of financing the buyout, plus taxes
- higher depreciation occurs in the first few years. It results in larger total payments for a relatively shorter time frame on the road
- when a lease needs to be broken before the expiry, the costs can be as high as all the outstanding lease payments still left. After all, the lease was based on a fixed term. It calculated the depreciation over a pre-set period of time and was expecting to have payments made over a much longer time.

Chapter 6

Lines of Credit

Not too many years ago, a properly trained and capable lending officer, often known in the community, and established in the branch, would actually become involved in the application for a loan. They would consult and interview, take a credit application, review the reason for the loan and even offer a little financial advice or insight.

But internal costs to lend small amounts, one loan at a time, were becoming very costly when compared to potential interest income. And yet most people just wanted a three or five thousand-dollar loan and were quite creditworthy. The alternative for most smaller loans was to add it on a charge card, or an overdraft, which was unacceptable to most customers due to their high interest rates. Lenders certainly wanted to retain their clients, but also wanted to make each account profitable at the lowest possible expense. The most efficient solutions for them and their clients became a line of credit that has always been widely used by corporations to finance their ever-changing inventory and accounts receivable.

In some ways, a line of credit is almost like a chequing account. It becomes a permanently useable loan set up for a fixed amount and continuously available and open similar to a credit card, but with much more attractive rates. It allows the customer the freedom to use any or all of it for whatever reason or amount at any time. In fact, lines of credit come with cheques to be able to access them, just as if there was actual money in an account.

The application process is the same as other bank loans; it's just that you won't need to see your neighbourhood banker any more when you want another loan or to re-finance for a larger amount. On the other hand, it can be like a permanent loan. It allows a one-time set up and turns the discipline of payments over to the priorities of the consumer. A $5,000 line of credit can be used for any reason at any time. Just like the limit on a credit card, this approved amount is in place and its use is up to the individual. When the balance is zero, there is no interest. When a part of it is used, interest is charged on the amount actually owing from that day, until it is paid in full. Minimum payments are usually three percent of the balance outstanding, and interest is charged only on that amount. The interest rate is set as a percentage above the prime rate, depending on the credit score, so as rates change the interest amount will fluctuate as well.

Lines of credit are very convenient and create total control over their use. They are also very flexible in their repayment requirements – for better or worse. As long as the minimum payments are made, any additional funds go straight to the principal. The consumer has become the loan officer that decides each month how much to pay and how quickly to pay it off. It is certainly one of the least costly and most convenient forms of credit. Some advertisements call them financial freedom, and it is for many consumers. But like anything else, it has to be managed well and kept under control.

Once the line of credit is established, the former structure of loan applications, calculating debt ratios and other steps are no longer needed. The poor customer has now been made the loan officer. With no training and limited knowledge, the holder of the credit line might be well on the way to permanent debt between this account and his or her credit cards. While it can be paid off at any time, it does not have any fixed repayment schedule over a term of three or four years, as typical loans do. The chance to make small monthly payments and the financial security of having it available continuously is a big advantage – but it can also be a big risk for those same reasons. Lines of credit are established in two different ways:

Unsecured Lines

For smaller amounts and creditworthy customers, lines of credit are the norm. They will generally be in the range of $3,000 to $10,000. These usually range from two to six percent above prime, depending on the credit worthiness of the customer and charge payments of at least three percent on the outstanding balance. It creates a small principal repayment each month, in addition to covering the interest charges.

Unsecured simply means that no actual collateral is pledged. It may be harder to obtain, but only requires an above-average credit rating and sufficient income to service the debt. With slogans such as never get another loan, 24-hour access and be your own credit manager, every financial institution now offers them. Different names, but identical in how they are established or function.

Secured Lines

Every lender loves having something tangible for collateral since it reduces their risk if something goes wrong and payments aren't made. For many accounts, the collateral is the equity in a house. When the amount is 80 percent or less of the appraised value, the interest is charged at prime rate, since there is very little risk. The monthly payments are interest only without ever having to pay money toward the principal. That is just fine with the lender, if the truth be known. For them, the longer the debt is outstanding, the more interest they earn.

Their set-up does involve some one-time fees similar to those of a mortgage. The financial institution will require a formal appraisal of the home to calculate the value and equity. Since a lien is pledged against the property, the documentation for the borrowing needs to be executed with a lawyer in the same way as normal mortgages. When you know the value of the home, the calculation of the maximum available is easy:

Example actual appraised value of residence	$200,000
Multiply by the maximum advance of 75%	X 0.80
Equals maximum total amount	= $ 160,000
Subtract the entire current mortgage balance(s)	- $ 132,000
Equals the maximum amount available for the line of credit	= $ 28,000

 A line of credit creates long-term debt from short-term bills and spends the equity in your house.

Another major consideration is the interest charge. Any reference to prime, or prime plus, means that the rate is adjusted and calculated monthly. In periods of rising rates, this becomes a windfall for lenders who immediately get to pass on those higher rates – but a greater risk for the borrower. When interest rates rise on a minimal overdraft, it is reasonably easy to stop using them. When it happens on a large line of credit, few people have the resources to pay the full balance immediately to avoid any rate increase. In the case of credit lines with larger balances it leaves only two options, either absorbing the increased interest costs or to re-mortgage (yes, the rates have already increased by that point) to lock in the amount owing before it (potentially) becomes worse.

Using a Credit Line for Your Mortgage

A line of credit can also be secured when the mortgage is already over 80 percent. It will give the lender collateral but at a higher rate. The time to consider a line of credit is when looking for a mortgage. As there is a significant cost difference between a conventional mortgage with 20 percent or more as a down payment, or a high-ratio mortgage, a line of credit can be an option to bridge the shortfall. This alternative will avoid the requirement of insurance on high ratio mortgages.

For example: You are five percent short of the full down payment on a $200,000 mortgage. Do you take a high ratio mortgage or a separate line of credit? Since the down payment is $10,000 short of qualifying for a conventional mortgage, it creates two choices:

Use the 15 percent down payment and add CMHC insurance of 1.75% at a cost of $3,500 plus their application fee. Maybe it's "only" $3,500, but over a standard 25-year mortgage, this total cost will be more than $6,500.

The alternate is to make up the $10,000 from a separate line of credit. Payments will be three percent per month or $300 to start. The total cost will be much less if the line of credit is cleared off within a reasonable time. For one year, the interest is $384, two years makes it $746 and even a three-year term is $1,116. All three terms are much less expensive than the total cost of mortgage insurance charged over 25 years.

The line of credit uses a seven percent rate as an example and can reduce your mortgage costs. It might mean taking a longer term or lower mortgage payment to make the debt-load work, but most mortgages do allow a 10 or 20 percent increase during the term. If it works as an alternative, always make paying off this line of credit your first priority and then take the extra funds to increase your mortgage payments.

The Risks of Using Them

Their big drawback is the discipline required to re-pay the balance. It is well known that only about half of credit card users pay off their balances each month. While no specific statistics are available from financial institutions, obviously a much lower number actually clear their lines of credit with any frequency.

A line of credit will never match the logical term of a loan. To stress this again, it is easy to fall into the trap of using a line of credit for longer-term debt than it should be. It is solely up to the individual to pay back the amount in a very disciplined and structured manner. After all, more and more consumers use these credit lines for large ticket purchases such as boats, cards, RVs and even their RRSP contributions.

A boat that someone plans to keep for four years should properly be financed for four years. This creates equity and saves interest. If a cheque is written on a credit line there is still financing in place. It is now up to the user to assure sufficiently high payments are made to pay the balance over an appropriate time. If not, the boat may be quite depreciated,

Make sure to match the length of time you'll take paying it back to the life of the purchase.

while the balance continues to linger well beyond the useful life of the asset. Or worse, since there is nobody monitoring the reason the line of credit was used, the boat can simply be sold and the money spent on something else, while the account continues to accumulate interest and eat up monthly payments.

In the example of a $5,000 boat paid through a line of credit at seven percent, you can: Pay three percent minimum payments each month, which start at $150 (3 percent of $5,000). But these payments will keep getting less and less each month. Making the minimum payments will take 148 months, over 12 years to pay off and costs $1,165 in total interest.

Instead, pay the $150 in fixed installments each month (no matter what the payment says at the bottom of each statement). Now it will take only 38 months and results in only $576 interest.

Another frequently heard story and horrible example is a loan taken for a long awaited, probably well-earned vacation. A personal loan should, logically, be set up over 12 monthly payments. The same amount drawn on a line of credit is still a debt, but now nobody is assuring this is paid off before the next vacation arrives. Since there is no requirement for a specific payback, only the three percent minimum (or interest only if fully secured) has to be made. On $1,000 at seven percent, the vacation will actually take seven years to pay.

Most times when the amount warrants, a personal loan can be obtained at comparable rates. These loans can be both fixed rate and fixed payments of interest and principal. Best of all, they will retire the debt over a specific period. It leaves the line of credit available for emergencies or short-term needs and separates loan obligations for more expensive ticket items.

Credit lines work best for those desiring flexibility or access to the total amount over a longer period of time, drawing funds over several months during a renovation project or other needs where money is required gradually. Interest is then only paid for the amount already drawn (used) and allows the flexibility of repayment terms at the customers' choosing.

Another wise use for credit lines can be the consolidation of smaller bills. This generally includes consolidating credit cards, store accounts and other bills with higher rates. Consolidating these by paying them off with a line of credit almost always results in significant interest savings. This is especially true with credit cards that can charge triple the rates when compared to a line of credit. Generally consolidations do require an above average credit rating or collateral. They are a danger sign to financial institutions since they take a number of smaller risk loans from different companies, and combine all of them into one account, at the risk of the lender making the consolidation loan.

This is another way that a financial professional or a loan officer can be helpful. While there is an immediate relief in only having one bill now, the amount after consolidation can be quite large. Interest charges may be less, but the total can quickly add up. It will always require the discipline to maintain larger monthly payments to also pay off the credit line. The point of

A consolidation hasn't paid off your other bills. It has just moved them around.

a consolidation is only achieved if the credit cards are cancelled and not run up again, since their old balance is now simply hidden in the credit line debt. A great quote came from Robin Leonard when he wrote: "Sometimes it's a good idea to borrow from Peter to pay Paul – but it depends on who Peter is."

There is no doubt that any line of credit is far preferable to credit card debt, cash advances or most types of consumer loans. It does come with the proviso that they are paid off with discipline. Not many people would simply skip a loan payment, or from time to time decide to pay only the interest for a while. Yet that is very possible on a line of credit.

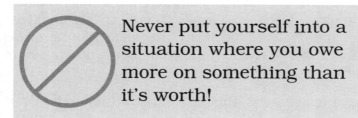

Never put yourself into a situation where you owe more on something than it's worth!

When the monthly statement arrives, the only tip a lender gives you is to outline the absolute minimum amount. The rest is up to you. Have you been trained just to pay what they have asked for? That only works for your cable TV bill and your utilities. Nowhere does it state the time it will take to pay the full balance at minimum payment. If it is secured – even worse – as it's possible to pay interest only and never a dime toward the principal. Wouldn't it be a rude awakening if each statement came with a warning: "At your balance of $1,020 with minimum payments it will take approximately 84 months to pay in full?"

Chapter 7

Mortgages

There are really only two ways to buy a house - with your money or someone else's money. What would baby boomers of the past generations have done without the huge tax-free equity they now have in their principal residence? This only came about through hard beginnings, a down payment scraped together or borrowed, and a mortgage.

Mortgage is a noun from the French word *mort* meaning "dead" and *gage* which is to "pledge." This is a pledge that (only) dies when the debt is paid in full. It is the charge or lien against the property – just a long-term loan with your home as collateral.

Obtaining a mortgage is almost a dance – the lender wants the largest return for the least amount of risk while the borrower wants the most generous terms at the lowest rate, for the longest time.

Surveys show that about 20 percent of Canadians plan to purchase a house in the next few years. Some will upgrade to a bigger home while many will become first-time homeowners with help of a mortgage. This is an area where it really pays to shop around, spending at least the same amount of energy as finding that perfect house or condo. After all, wouldn't you negotiate on the price of the house? Well, that savings could be a drop in the bucket compared to what a mortgage can cost – or save you. When signing the mortgage you are probably just happy to get on with it – but down the road any restrictions should not come back to haunt you when you're willing and able to pre-pay parts of the mortgage or to increase your payments.

Getting your mortgage comes in various stages. The *before* window of starting to look for a house and the *getting ready* stage. The *during* stage when the purchase and mortgage are really happening and the *after* stage of making payments and pre-payment options you've agreed to – or signed away.

 You'd be surprised if you knew how many mortgage lenders would love to compete for your business.

Shopping for a Mortgage

Mortgage shopping has nothing to do with convenience, and where you currently bank is irrelevant. It's not as if you're ever going to visit your mortgage company for coffee. Whether they are located across town or in a different province, what matters are their rate and terms. The payments will be debited from your account no matter where you live or bank.

When it comes to taking on a debt of this size and length, it is not the time to be lazy, complacent, or just consider convenience. It will take some work, but it is worth it. On an $200,000 purchase you might negotiate a $5,000 or $10,000 discount, but a one percent reduction in rate will save over $33,000. That should be enough incentive to do your homework.

What you are looking for is a pre-approved mortgage. After all, once a purchase offer is in place, the panic is on and the meter is running. At that point, there is very little time for the luxury of shopping around. This way, lenders can compete for your business while there is less stress and time constraints.

A pre-approval is simply a written commitment by the financial institution. It will outline your down payment and set the maximum you quality for, along with a rate guarantee, usually for 60 or 90 days, before the mortgage has to be in place. If rates go up during that time – you are protected and will only pay the guaranteed rate, not the new rates. Should they decrease, you will receive the new lower rate. It does not mean you are obligated to deal with that lender if a better deal comes along. They are simply giving you a written offer of what they can and will do.

Any pre-approval supplies a secure framework of all the figures but does not mean you necessarily want a mortgage of that size. It is only the maximum you can qualify for. Yes, there is fine print. It is always subject to completing an appraisal of the property after you have found a house and have signed the offer to purchase. It sure beats having found a house and then sweating if the mortgage will go through, whether or not there is enough income to qualify, or to start tracking down the T4s and other records needed to complete the paperwork.

Anyone can do most of the pre-approval process. Just complete the income and debt load calculations from the charts at the back of the book. This will give you the maximum amount of a mortgage payment possible. Lenders look at the total debt service ratio (TDSR) vs. your gross income, which cannot exceed 40 percent. With this figure, use a mortgage rate range and look up the mortgage payments in the back for various terms and the payment frequency you desire. For example:

Gross monthly income with your partner	$4,000
40% of that towards payments is	$1,600
Deduct total list of current payments	$ 320
Is total monthly payment available for mortgage	$1,280

For example, if mortgage rates are around five percent, use the schedule at the end of the book to calculate the approximate amount you can afford. With some trial and error, you will quickly find the maximum amount will be about $220,000, which is a payment of $1,280. Added to this is the amount of the down payment and you will have the maximum amount of the house price after negotiation.

In addition to knowing the amount you qualify for and the amount of down payment you've saved, there is more. There are all the other costs and surprises you will need to anticipate when purchasing a house, over and above any down payment:

- Inspection charges – if you are choosing to have a company do a full inspection as part of the purchase process.

- Legal fees – which include disbursements to register the mortgage, courier charges and lawyer's fees. As these vary quite a bit, it pays to shop around. Most lawyers will quote their fee plus disbursements based on purchase price.

- Real Estate/Land transfer taxes – some provinces charge a percentage of the total transaction amount.

- Appraisal fee – an independent assessment of the property value required by your lender to assure the property is of sufficient value to cover their mortgage. If you have less than a 20 percent down payment, the CMHC fee will include the cost of the appraisal.

- Tax adjustment – tax is billed only once a year. You will be responsible for the adjustment of tax between you and the seller – you are be paying tax for the part of the calendar year you will own the property.

- Surveyor certificate – this is a form required by lenders to verify that the property is correctly and legally situated on the lot and that zoning, any garage or additions, decks, etc. confirm with municipal zoning. Some lenders require a new one on each application, while others will accept a previous survey certificate from the seller of the property.

- Moving costs – of course, this will always depend on how far you are moving, how much stuff there is and how many friends and family you can count on.

- Interest adjustment amount – most lenders require their mortgage payments on the first of each month. You do need to pay the interest from the day of the mortgage to the first of the following month. This is the interest adjustment. You will be safe (and a little high) if you take your mortgage payment divided by 30 days in a month times the number of days left in the month to calculate the amount owing.

- Home insurance – before the mortgage is advanced, you will need to place insurance on the property that shows the mortgage company as loss payable (they will receive first right to the funds if there is a claim). Your insurance broker will have a software program to walk through the calculations of the insurance coverage. The amount will not be the same as your purchase price – in case of a fire, the land and its value will still be intact and thus not need to be insured.

- Mortgage insurance – is the CMHC fee for high ratio mortgages. You may choose to pay this premium or have it added to the mortgage amount.

- Life or accident & sickness insurance – either are always an optional coverage. Premiums are on a monthly basis and added to your payment. You can also purchase this after the mortgage is already in place and can also cancel it at any point. But mortgage insurance is expensive and very limiting. It is designed to protect lenders and only pays out the mortgage. While it will leave your family with a paid off home, chances are they may be forced to sell it in order to make other payments. A term life policy, even for the same amount as the mortgage, is actually payable to your family. It gives them a choice of paying the mortgage or continuing with the payments and having the funds available for other bills. Either way, it creates financial freedom instead of possibly more pain and loss.

 Skip the costly mortgage life insurance and get a term life policy instead.

- Utility hook-up and transfer charges.

- Renovations or improvements that need to be made before you can move into the property.

- Other costs – especially if you are moving from a rental premise. This can include the typical homeowner starter kit of lawn mower, drapes, allpiances or furniture.

Just as finding the perfect house comes with a gotta-have list and a like to have list, the same should be the case for a mortgage. There are always features that will be more important than others are, although the main issue will always be the interest rate. After that, you will need to decide what term and total amortization suit your budget. Aggressive enough that you will save a significant amount of interest and conservative enough where it will still be in your comfort zone and allow you to sleep at night. A mortgage should not be an afterthought when shopping for a home. The interest paid on the mortgage will be much higher than the original purchase price, so it needs to be one of the first things to deal with, not the last.

Let's face it, all banks match any rate changes within hours. But these rates are only benchmarks used to calculate penalties for early termination, they are no longer the rates customers will be charged. Yet rates can vary by over one percent between companies. Lenders are clearly promoting this fact through advertising wording such as best rates or similar slogans that will be much less than their posted rates.

What Happens When You Apply?

The job of all lenders is to evaluate and manage risk and for mortgages that involves a lot of questions and paperwork. There are also restrictions that a mortgage cannot exceed 75 percent of the appraised value. Any advance beyond this amount is subject to approval by the mortgage insurer who assumes the risk over that amount.

Lenders will want all the information on you (or you and your partner). If you already have an offer to purchase a property, they will obtain information on the property as well. The first step is to complete a credit application and obtain the backup documentation. Requirements vary between lenders, but your homework must include bringing along at least:

- The last two years of T-4s or the first page of the last two tax returns to verify gross income. When possible, supply your Notice of Assessment, the tax form confirming your return in summary. It also verifies that there are no taxes in arrears as lenders rarely have an interest in lending money to anyone with an outstanding tax bill.

- A letter from your employer to confirm employment, gross income, and whether you are full-time permanent or part time.

- Your last pay stub from the current year, which should show the income year-to-date.

- A list of assets and liabilities. Complete the schedule in the back of the book, feel free to copy it to take with you as it will save you a significant number of questions and time.

- Receipts for any loans, credit cards or other bills you have paid in full over the past couple of months. Credit bureau information is up to 60 days behind. When lenders calculate debts, it is helpful to have up-to-date information if some bills have now been paid down or paid in full.

- The completed and signed offer to purchase, if you have already found a house, as well the name of the lawyer to use for the mortgage papers and disbursement of funds.

- Proof of down payment – the source of money. Lenders need to be sure that it isn't from borrowed funds, but has actually been saved. A copy of your passbook, term deposit or bank machine receipt will be enough.

If you are self-employed, this becomes more extensive. You may need three years financial statements from your company as well as your personal returns to prove you are paying yourself enough money to make the payments. After all, it is you purchasing the property, so it involves judging your personal income and not that of the company.

Open or Closed?

Mortgages are broadly defined in two categories:

- Open – which gives you the option of repaying all or parts of the mortgage at any point without penalty. The advantage is total freedom and flexibility. An open mortgage also allows you to convert it to a fixed rate mortgage at any time.

- Closed – are mortgages locked in or restricted for a specific period of time. Pre-payment privileges are limited and vary between lenders. Actual closed mortgages are much less common these days. The competitive nature of the business means most still allow the opportunity to pay an extra 10 or 20 percent toward the mortgage. Their interest rates are generally lower, since lenders have some guarantee of what they will make in interest (profit) over a fixed time period.

Prepare your list of mortgage choices in order of importance and share them with your potential lenders.

- Limited open/closed are the most common type. These include specific pre-payment options and at least a small amount of flexibility. They are often advertised as 10 plus 10 or even 20 plus 20. These so-called step up features mean that a lump sum can be paid and the payment can also be increased by that same percentage. The rest of the mortgage is closed and would attract a pre-payment penalty if the house is sold or the mortgage paid off for another reason.

Amortization and Term

Amortization is the entire time frame over which the outstanding amount will be repaid. Since mortgages are not fixed for the entire 20 or 25 years, there are rate adjustment steps along the way. Would you lend someone a large amount of money and guess what interest rates will do more than 20 years from now? This is the same question lenders ask as they look to match their deposits taken in with their mortgages lent out. Unlike the United States where these fixed rate mortgages are available, generally the longest time in Canada is seven to 10 years. These are called the mortgage terms at which time the mortgage is renewed, paid out or transferred. It is the point when the lender can re-adjust the rate but also the time when the borrower has a range of options without attracting a penalty.

The entire length of your mortgage (this amortization) is one of the main places where you can save significant interest. Not many years ago it was common to see almost all mortgages for the standard 25 years. Consumers today are more aware of the total cost to pay a mortgage in full. It is more common these days to have the total amortization as long as 40 years or short as you choose, based on the payment selected and a range of payment frequencies.

Common Mortgages Types

Conventional Mortgage

A conventional mortgage is one that has at least a 20 percent down payment of the purchase price or appraisal, whichever is less. Any lender handles this type of mortgage directly without requirements for additional mortgage insurance. To them, it is a very low risk mortgage, as there is a significant down payment.

High Ratio Mortgage

High ratio is the term for amounts over 80 percent of the appraisal or purchase price. As this finances an amount beyond a conventional mortgage, legislation requires lenders to have these insured against potential losses due to their lower amount of equity, which is discussed at the end of this section.

Second Mortgages

A second mortgage is simply another loan against the property over an above the first mortgage. On default or foreclosure, proceeds are paid first to the primary lien holder, and only the leftover amount goes to the second mortgage. This makes them a bigger risk, and the reason for their higher rate. They are commonly used in two situations:

The first is the chance to buy a house with a great low mortgage already in place. Most are assumable and it can sometimes be quite advantageous to take over an existing mortgage at rates no longer available. Depending on the amount, it can leave a shortfall between the purchase price and the amount of this mortgage. Rather than passing up this existing one, it may make sense to add a second mortgage for the shortfall of funds. While they are at a higher rate, a second mortgage (or line of credit) can still be less costly. Of course, this will always depend on how attractive the existing first mortgage really is.

 Assuming an existing mortgage is always your option. This should only be done if it makes overall financial sense.

Another scenario might make it desirable to avoid mortgage penalties. During the term of a current mortgage, refinancing means paying a penalty. The option always exists of re-mortgaging at a higher blended rate or to pay a pre-payment penalty. If both of these options come at a higher cost, a second and shorter-term mortgage may be an alternative as it leaves the first mortgage untouched.

Because of the risk, these can often be double the interest rate of a first mortgage. The amount advanced depends on the lender, but will generally be up to 90 or 95 percent of the appraised value. It involves doing some simple comparison math to calculate the total payback on re-mortgaging the first compared to the cost of a second mortgage.

Condominium Mortgage

A condominium project starts off with a mortgage by the developer. It covers the entire project and all apartments and common areas of the complex. When one unit is sold, it is removed from the blanket mortgage so that clear title can be passed to the purchaser. At that point the developer pays back a portion of the blanket mortgage to his lender until all the units are sold and his mortgage is completely discharged. Each owner of a condominium has title to their own unit, as well as some type of undivided interest in the common area.

Fixed Rate Mortgage

As the word implies, this is an interest rate locked-in for a specific period of time, ranging from six months to 10 years. On fixed rate mortgages, the payments and interest rate will stay the same throughout the term.

Variable Rate Mortgage

This type has interest rates that change from time-to-time with market conditions. The rate adjustments correspond with fluctuations in the prime rate, which will affect the floating or variable mortgage rate. When rates are falling, it means a reduced interest rate right along with it. When rates are on the increase, however, the mortgage rate keeps going up as well. While payments remain fixed, the amount applied to principal will change. Payments have interest deducted first, so less interest means more to principal and vice-versa.

Mortgage Insurance

Canada Mortgage and Housing Corporation (CMHC) is a government agency that administers and funds mortgage insurance programs to protect lenders against default. It is mandatory and charged on any mortgage over 80 percent of the appraised value. It protects lenders when they make a mortgage loan with less than a 20 percent down payment for so called high ratio mortgages. GE Capital is the other national mortgage insurer, however CMHC has the lions share of the market with almost $300 billion of insured mortgages. Minimum requirements changed in early 2004 when CMHC announced they would allow no down payment mortgages. This still requires proof of sufficient funds available for closing costs as well as what they term a good credit standing. CMHC controls other factors as well, ranging from final approval of the credit application and a maximum property value (you can purchase), plus the mortgage amount (they will lend).

CMHC Charges:

The mortgage insurance cost will be an application fee plus a percentage charge, depending on the amount of the mortgage:

Mortgage Advance	Percentage fee of mortgage amount
To 100%	3.1%
To 97%	2.9%
To 95%	2.75%
To 90%	2.0%
To 85%	1.75%
To 80%	1.0%

Additional costs will apply for certain mortgage types such as variable rates or progressive advances where you are building a home.

For 40 year terms there is an additional CMC surcharge of 0.6%. Consequently, for someone with a five percent down payment the total fee would be 3.35%. On a $200,000 mortgage the total premium is $6,700, an additional $67 each month, and translates to $17,500 over the life of the loan.

Mortgage fees can be paid up front or included in the monthly payments.

Mortgage Rates

Nobody knows with any certainty what interest rates will do in the future. Experts can make educated predictions, but they are not making your payments. Whether you're deciding on a new mortgage term or the length of your renewal, it is advisable to ask some experts and read a few financial forecasts. But at the end of the day, only you can decide your risk tolerance or comfort level. Can you afford to gamble on a shorter term and lower rate that will have you renewing sooner rather than later? Or are you are more comfortable with a long-term stable mortgage and a safe budget that will ride out any fluctuations in the meantime?

Surveys by CIBC found that almost two-thirds of consumers felt that their best option was to secure a fixed rate mortgage while less than 30 percent were comfortable with a variable-rate option. Moshe Milevsky of York University conducted a study that covered a 50 year period and found that a $100,000 mortgage over 15 years would have cost $22,000 less on a variable rate mortgage rather than five-year terms.

Mortgage interest is calculated semi-annually, not in advance. It only specifies how often the interest is actually calculated. The more often – the more costly, but it has no connection to how often the payments are made. The term 'not in advance' means that it is important to remember you are making your mortgage payment at the end of each period. A landlord collects rent at the beginning of the month, while the mortgage payment is applied to the month that has just passed. The actual interest on mortgages is charged as part of each payment. Whether this is made monthly or more frequently, the lender will always take their interest first before applying the balance of what's left to the principal.

Short-Term or Long?

These are questions that have a different answer for different sets of needs, risk tolerances, budgets and comfort levels.

Shorter-term interest rates are mainly as a result of the early 1980's. When rates approached 20 percent, not many people wanted a mortgage for a very long term in the hope that rate reductions were just around the corner. Variable rate mortgages allowed the adjustment of interest more frequently, sometimes as often as once a month. It created more flexibility and helped when rates (eventually) came down. But they also passed the risk of rate changes directly onto the borrower. After all, nothing feels better than to have a long term mortgage when rates are rising – or having a floating rate that keeps coming down every month as interest rates drop and drop. But both come with a risk and reward scale that is a personal choice. Longer-term mortgages can provide:

- ease of long-term budgeting
- stability
- peace of mind without worrying about possible rate changes
- slightly higher rates – but avoiding any short-term spikes
- minimally higher payments

Shorter-term mortgages can provide:

- a shorter term
- slightly lower payments
- a lower interest rate
- more exposure to rate changes – since your renewal will be more frequent – for better or worse
- increased flexibility – if you are considering potentially re-mortgaging or selling as there will be no penalties at the end of your term

The Latest, Greatest – Worst

One of the worst financial imports from the U.S. is the recently developed 40-year mortgage. Yet, according to a recent RBC Homeowner Survey, almost half of all first-time homebuyers are choosing this term which can take a dream home and turn it into a financial prison.

A $250,000 mortgage for 40-years stretches the term an additional 15 years in order to lower payments by $235, compared to the standard 25-years. Focusing only on payments, that may seem like a good idea at the time, but at a very high cost of over $177,000 in extra interest. After ten long years of payments, barely $20,000 of principal has been paid and the total payments add up $660,000. Since only net income can go to payments, even in a 30% tax bracket someone would have to earn just under $1 million just to pay off this mortgage! As with any borrowing, just because you can – doesn't mean you should.

Before signing a mortgage that will not be paid off before you die of old age, could you:

• Purchase a home for a lower selling price?

• Pay off one of your current bills to get your budget in line?

• Save a little longer or a little more to increase the down payment?

• Would your parents help out? NOT with a loan, as that's just making something bad – worse, but with a gift of some down-payment to help you avoid a large financial trap?

The Questions You've Gotta Ask

There are some basic questions you should be ready with when in search of your mortgage:

• What mortgage options do you have available?

• What are your posted rates or what will you offer me?

• Will you lower the rate if I bring you other banking business?

- Do you charge an application fee – if so, what does it include?

- Do you need a new survey certificate or is an existing one acceptable?

- What is the time frame you will need to approve my mortgage? (A pre-approval if you have your proper paperwork with you should take around a day – if you have your offer to purchase and are ready to obtain the mortgage, it will be at least two or three additional days to obtain the appraisal of the property).

Not having the answers is a reason to start asking questions, not a signal to stop!

- What payment options are there? Weekly, bi-weekly, etc.

- Can I change my payments from monthly to bi-monthly or another method without penalty at a later date?

- If I share your lawyer, will you be able to offer a fee break?

- What are the penalties for paying off the mortgage before the end of the term?

- What are my pre-payment options? Can I add 10 percent to my payments at any time; can I pay a lump sum on it on each anniversary date without penalty?

- What is your term for pre-approved rate guarantee – 60 - 90 days or longer?

- I have less than a 20 percent down payment, what are my total CMHC fees and charges?

- What are your mortgage renewal fees?

- Do you have a skip payment option if I absolutely need it? (Allowing you to skip a monthly payment and having it added to the mortgage balance)

- Is the mortgage assumable should if I sell the house?

- What frequency of mortgage payments do you have available to choose from?

- Is the mortgage portable (where you are able to take your mortgage with you to another home should you sell the first property)?

- Do I have to pay my property tax with the mortgage? (you may wish to for budgeting or choose to pay this yourself each year)

Mortgage Obligations

Your obligations are spelled out in many pages of legal size documents that you pay a lawyer to walk you through and also outline when default occurs. Most are standard mortgage terms and really mean you have to:

- Pay the payments on time each month – every month.

- Make your property tax payments when they are due (if not included in your payment to the lender already).

- Stay within the rules, zoning and by-laws for the house. If it is zoned residential – don't put a small engine repair business into your garage.

- Keep up the condition so the value does not go down and jeopardize the lender – nobody is interested in deciding whether you want to re-paint the bathroom, but they do want you to fix structural damage and the likes which have a significant impact on the value.

- If you have a second mortgage keep both up-to-date. They are inter-connected as it is the same property.

- Keep it insured – adequate insurance protects the lender in the event of a fire. They have the mortgage and want to make sure they are covered by insurance to get the value of the property back to where it was.

Changing Your Mortgage

Unless a mortgage is open to pay whatever you choose without penalty, or is at the end of the term, refinancing will involve penalties. They are charges which lenders collect if you want to pay off your mortgage early, or are selling the house and the mortgage is not being assumed by the new purchaser.

As you were locked in to a fixed term, the lender will be looking for this penalty. It can range from three months of interest to the interest differential, the larger amount is usually charged. The differential is what the lender can get from a new borrower today versus what you are currently paying. If your rate is seven percent on a mortgage from a couple of years ago and today's rate is six, you will be charged the difference of this one percent for what is left on your term. Conversely, if your rate is lower – they don't mind having you pay the mortgage and the penalty will be three months of interest.

The shorter the time remaining on your term, the less costly and more attractive early renewal or re-mortgaging becomes. In the event you want to re-mortgage, there will still be a penalty. It will just be blended into the new rate. Re-mortgaging actually consists of paying the old mortgage and starting a totally new one for a different amount, different terms and other features.

This generally occurs in two common situations. The first is paying off some other bills, incorporating renovations into the mortgage, or a desire to take advantage of lower rates. To increase a mortgage, the lender will do another appraisal to verify that there is sufficient equity (room) in your house to add this additional amount. Refinancing waves can be a major stimulant in the overall economy. In the past number of years it has been a measurable factor as people with equity in their home have frequently taken out this equity to consolidate other debts. It also frees up cash flow that allow for more borrowing which is often invested in renovations, upgrades, and a host of other stimulants for the economy.

Unfortunately, these will not receive the lowest available rates. Assuming you have a closed mortgage, you are still locked into your existing rate. So before you get excited about the new rates out in the world, have a talk with your lender. It will take no more than a couple of minutes to get the full facts, figures and options if this is worth pursuing.

What you will receive is a blended rate. The lender combines the current rate for the rest of the term with the new rate over a longer time period. For example: If you have one-year left and are willing to sign a new five-year term, it will probably makes sense financially. However, if you have a long period remaining on the old rate, a new five-year term may not be sufficiently long to make an impact on your payment. In either event, it never hurts to ask and explore all options.

At the end of any mortgage term many people consider renovations or upgrades to the home. This is often termed good borrowing when the money is invested back into the house for things that tend to increase in value. The ultimate goal is always to be mortgage free, so it is not the only way to pay for renovations:

- with savings – by paying cash
- personal loan (fixed installment loan)
- home equity line of credit (up to 80 percent of the appraised value less mortgage amount still owing)
- re-mortgage (if you are at the end of the term or have an open mortgage where there are no penalties)
- a separate personal line of credit

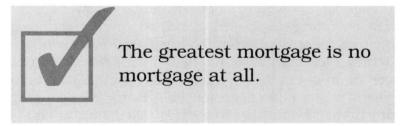

The greatest mortgage is no mortgage at all.

At the end of each term, the mortgage is due and must be paid in full or renewed with new rates and terms. Generally, your lender will offer to renew your mortgage. Why wouldn't they? Everybody wants to keep their customers. You will be mailed the renewal offer a couple of months before the expiration.

Receiving the renewal should not mean just signing and mailing it back. You are being offered a renewal at posted rates available at the time and have until maturity to decide.

Shop around for the best available terms and rates with other lenders just as you would for a pre-approval. To switch, you will have a discharge fee from your current lender, a new appraisal and legal fees, but most lenders will gladly pay these to get your business. The process of switching lenders is fairly painless but does involve some work and time, so make sure it is going to save you money. You can also:

- Pay off your mortgage. You are at the maturity date so there will be no penalty or pre-payment charges.
- Pay down your mortgage. At each renewal you have the option to pay any additional money without penalty.

At this point, you may also want to re-visit the amount of payments you are comfortable with. Since you know the balance shown on your renewal form, just re-calculate what you choose your new payment to be, for a shorter time, from the charts at the back of the book. If you are signing for a longer term closed mortgage again – it's now or never as the saying goes.

Paying More – Paying More Often

Even if it is not renewal time, most closed mortgages still have some type of pre-payment privileges. Standard terms tend to be 10-10 or even 20-20 clauses, which refer to both a lump sum at each anniversary date, and this same percentage as an increase in payments.

Paying more can also be a decision to change the frequency of payments. Standard terms are generally monthly – but it is not the only option. Increasing the frequency is THE most effective way to reduce your total interest. No trick, no gimmick, no catch – more money going towards the principal, more often means less interest – it really is that simple. Payments can be made in six different ways:

- Monthly: 12 payments per year
- Semi-monthly: 24 payments per year
  (Monthly payment times 12 months divided by 24 for two payments per month)
- Bi-weekly: 26 payments per year
  (Monthly payment times 12 months divided by 26 for a payment every two weeks)
- Weekly: 52 payments per year
  (Monthly payment times 12 divided by 52 for a payment every week)

You can also speed up two of these payment types:

- Accelerated Bi-weekly: 26 payments per year
  (monthly payment divided by two)
- Accelerated weekly: 52 payments per year
  (monthly payment divided by four)

This acceleration takes advantage of making extra payments over a year in small amounts. There will still be 26 (bi-weekly) or 52 (weekly) payments, but they are calculated differently to accelerate the payments.

For those options not shown in the charts at the back of the book, simply look up the monthly mortgage payment and calculate the payments as shown. It will make a big difference with very little effort. On a $200,000 mortgage at six percent the savings can be substantial:

Payment frequency	Amount	Amortization	Total interest	Interest saved
Monthly	$1,280	25 years	$183,881	$ 0
Semi-monthly	$ 640	24.9 years	$182,801	$ 1,084
Bi-weekly	$ 591	24.8 years	$181,040	$ 2,845
Weekly	$ 295	24.8 years	$180,552	$ 3,334
Accelerated Bi-weekly	$ 640	21.0 years	$148,675	$35,210
Accelerated Weekly	$ 320	20.9 years	$148,280	$35,605

Pre-paying a mortgage can be done in four ways:

- Pay extra money – if the mortgage permits.
- Reduce the amortization – length of mortgage (at renewal).
- Change the payments (i.e.: from monthly to weekly).
- Pay a lump sum (where permitted, usually at anniversary dates, or always at the renewal).

In case you need any more motivation to accelerate your payments, on a $200,000 at six percent here are the first five years of the mortgage:

Year #	Payments made	Amount to principal	Interest paid	Principal balance left
1	$15,355	$ 3,618	$11,737	$196,382
2	$15,355	$ 3,818	$11,537	$192,564
3	$15,355	$ 4,050	$11,304	$188,513
4	$15,355	$ 4,280	$11,075	$184,233
5	$15,355	$ 4,576	$10,779	$179,657
Totals:	$76,776	$20,344	$56,432	

Five long years are behind you with monthly payment of $1,280 and 74 percent of your payments have gone to interest.

A printed mortgage schedule lets you track your progress and motivates you to accelerate your payments.

Marketing a Magical Line Of Credit

One of the newest marketing tools to reach Canada is something called a money merge account, sometimes called an all-in-one account, or mortgage maximization software. In the U.S. it is sold with high pressure tactics for over $3,500 with the claim that you don't have to adjust your lifestyle at all, in order to pay off your mortgage years faster. The technical explanation of this is: Nonsense!

First, these lenders require you to set up a line of credit through which their software and payment maximization happens. The logic is to deposit your entire pay in this line of credit which will immediately go onto your mortgage balance and reduce the interest amount. Yet every person needs to pay bills and have money to live on. So the same day their paycheque is reducing the balance, every person takes money out of their account for utilities, groceries, this and that bill, and money to live on. For the vast majority of people, two days later perhaps $100 at most is left in the account. This extra $100 reduces the interest on the mortgage by 20 cents for the month!

With the second pay period, the same deposit is made, but the car payment, groceries, paying credit card payments and other money comes right back out of the line of credit account within a day or two, tops. If $200 is left at the end of the month, the extra interest savings amount to 20 cents from the first of the month pay and 10 cents from the middle of the month, or 30 cents in total.

However, this line of credit can also make things worse since it can also be used beyond any deposits and would result in more debt and interest than before!

Unfortunately, there is no magic pill for weight loss and no magic software that does not requires some lifestyle, budgeting or financial changes in order to pay off debt. It takes discipline and a game-plan and just sending in a few extra dollars each month accomplishes the same goal more effectively.

Chapter 8

Your Credit Bureau File

You can run, but you can't hide when it comes to your credit history. Even 30 years ago, a move across the country meant a good chance of leaving behind memories of credit problems that other lenders might not discover. Those days are long gone, much to the relief of all lenders.

Credit rating agencies are clearing houses for all credit information. If you don't know them – they certainly know you. In this country, it is usually Equifax Corporation and more recently, Trans Union. Both compete to sell reports to credit grantors across the country. The only effect for most consumers is that they now have two files with overlapping, or perhaps different, credit information with both these firms.

 **The credit bureaus have files on almost 25 million Canadians and sell over 40 million reports annually.**

Credit bureaus do not actively gather facts and reports. They collect information from banks, credit card issuers, finance companies, and almost all other lenders. They don't rate customers, but accumulate, sort and sell factual information as a central clearinghouse. At regular intervals, thousands of lenders simply exchange their data with the credit bureau, which instantly updates consumers' files with new accounts or information.

Anyone who lends money uses the credit bureaus as a source of information. Lenders receive a reduced price when purchasing a file in return for supplying their customer data on a regular basis. It means borrowers can stop wondering if maybe their late payment won't be noticed or reported, or their repossession might not show up. It will – without doubt – and quite quickly. After all, your credit rating is your factual and detailed financial reputation. Why should you care? Well, even something as simple as opening a chequing account with a bank card has the banks looking at your credit report. They're extending credit when they allow you to make withdrawals from your accounts without a hold on deposits through their machine.

What's In Your File

While files exist on millions of individuals, the content is nowhere near as exciting as many people think. It does not contain criminal records, asset information or office gossip. It is only a library, which catalogues and distributes factual and credit related information. Access is strictly limited to legitimate lenders who are also required to sign and adhere to a confidentiality agreement stating that they will not disclose the information obtained. In Canada it is recognized that someone's credit history is a very private matter and privacy laws are strictly adhered to in this industry because to the sensitive nature of the information. Additionally, in almost all Canadian provinces, a lender is required to have a signed application before they can ever proceed to obtain these reports. The information in files consist of various sections, which include:

- Identification section – to locate and identify an individual. It includes name, address, birth date and social insurance number.

- Inquiry information – listing the companies who have accessed the file and received the report in the past.

- Payment history – a factual record of previous or current accounts, including the amount borrowed, name of credit grantor, payment terms and how the account has been paid.

- Public records – included are bankruptcies, collections

and judgments as well as any secured loans and liens from certain provinces.

What's not included is almost any mortgage information. They are fully secured by the house and lenders are reluctant to share information that others can use to find out expiration dates in an effort to potentially steal their clients.

What A File Looks Like

A fictitious file will look somewhat like the following:

```
FN 00-007622-03-944       05/22/09
*CONSUMER,JAMES,L,KAREN      SINCE 02/12/86      FAD 05/12/09
    123 ANY STREET, VANCOUVER,BC  V7X 2T9
    222 DIFFERENT AVE, VANCOUVER,BC V8T 1T9
    BDS-08/10/62

*INQS-
04/19/09      BANK OF WINNIPEG          (604) 555-1221
03/19/08      RENT ME MANAGEMENT        (604) 555-3482
02/02/08      YR CREDIT UNION           (519) 555-9935

ES-INSTALLER, BC WORKALOT, VANCOUVER, BC,,$3200NV
EF-LABOURER, HOPE MANAGEMENT, VANCOUVER, BC

SUMMARY  02/99 - 05/09  NO-PR/01,FB-NO, TOTAL4,HC$0-14500,
1-ZERO, 2-ONES, 1-THREE

        RPTD  OPND  H/C  TRMS  BAL  P/D  RT  30/60/90  MR  DLA
*ABC VISA
        05/04 02/99 2140  59   1164  0   R1  03 01 00  35  05/09
AMOUNT IN H/C COLUMN IS CREDIT LIMIT

ALBERTA STORES INC
*     03/09 11/99 1000  10   200   0   R3  01 00 00  06  02/09

BANK OF ANYWHERE
*     05/09 09/02 14500 320 10740  0   R1  00 00 00  10  05/09

END OF REPORT
```

How To Read the Report

The first section is the place any computer looks for in finding the file, or matching to it when updating. It contains the name, spouses name followed by the 'since date' showing how long the consumer has had a file. It then lists the current plus previous address and birth date.

The second section shows the inquiry history. This is the summary of all lenders that have looked at the file and the dates of their inquiries.

The third reflects current and previous employment.

Section four is simply the summary of what is detailed from each of the creditors reporting. This is a Visa card opened (opnd) in February of 1999 and last reported (rptd) in May of 2009. It has a limit of $2,140 (H/C is high credit), minimum payments of $59 and a current balance of $1,164. The rating on this account is R1, which is explained in the next section. The 30/60/90 is also very important to lenders. It shows the number of times the account has been 30 days behind (three times), 60 days behind (once), and 90 or more days behind (never). The other two accounts are another small credit card and a bank loan with payments of $320 per month and a balance of $10,740.

The ratings show the current status of each account and are used throughout the industry as standard codes:

R-0 brand new accounts or not utilized
R-1 paying as agreed and within terms, on or before due date
R-2 one month past due, paying within 30-60 days
R-3 two months past due, paying within 60-90 days
R-4 three months past due, paying within 90-120 days
R-5 four months or more past due
R-6 no longer in use as a rating
R-7 payments within a consolidation or similar arrangement
R-8 a repossession
R-9 written off (as non-collectable) or placed for collection

How to Check Your Information

It is the right of any individual to review their own file. In fact, over half a million people do so each year. Unfortunately, most are likely to check just after they've been declined for credit. Like regular dental exams, it is a good idea to check the file at least every year or two in order to stay aware of the content and its accuracy. The process simply involves contacting either Equifax or Trans Union, whose information is listed in the back of the book, and giving them some basic information and identification for security purposes. After that, the report will be mailed directly with an instruction sheet on how to read the report written in user-friendly language. By law you are entitled to see your own credit report free of charge annually.

Mistakes To Look For

The most common errors are often housekeeping items on an ever changing and very fluid credit report. For the most part, these fall into the following categories:

- Spouse - This information can well be outdated or incorrect. While it is not part of the rating, it can easily be updated.

- Current address – This is generated by the last inquiry. Before the file is accessed, the credit grantor enters the basic information, which locates the correct file and also uses it as the latest update. This information may have been entered incorrectly and is also easy to correct.

- Current employer - Updates on the same premise as the address information. Every new inquiry kicks the current one into the former category.

- Paid out accounts not up-to-date – It is possible that a computer burp, oversights or other errors can cause a paid down or paid in full account, to be shown incorrectly. Any overstated payments and balances affect future borrowing. It causes the total debt and payment obligations to be inaccurate and too high. In these cases, the credit bureaus require proof that the account is paid in full and will contact the lender for verification. For these, it is best to contact the actual creditor to re-input their information accurately.

- Terminated credit cards – Similar to the above, credit card limits can also have a potential impact on future borrowing and should be updated in the same manner.

- Collections not cleared – While a collection will stay on file for some time there is a big difference between paid or still outstanding. These items are usually debts that have been turned over to a collection agency. Frequently, after they are paid, the credit file is not updated. It is critical that the status and balance are accurate. When a collection is outstanding, there will almost always be a requirement to pay it in full before most loans are approved.

- Secured loan not discharged – In some provinces, secured loans and chattels are shown in a separate section of the file. When they are paid off, the financial institution releases their lien of whatever was pledged for collateral. The credit bureaus also need to be up-to-date showing the loan is paid and the security is released.

- Good credit references missing – It is anyone's right to have their credit file complete as well as accurate. When a loan or other account is missing, it is worth a request that the item be included the file. It only makes sense to have as many positive references as possible, which includes accounts already paid in full over the past six years or less.

How to Fix Errors

While the error percentage is reasonably small, they do happen. This is not a matter of blaming anyone, since it starts with borrowers giving partial information, lenders not updating files correctly and ending with bureaus inserting it incorrectly. All files are the result of vast amounts of information gathered from many diverse sources. Horror stories from the United States and reported statistics of large percentages of inaccurate files simply aren't the case in this country. Yet even a one percent error rate means tens of thousands of individuals have a reason to review their files – before it becomes a problem.

The credit bureaus are under provincial legislation and most mandate disputes to be resolved within 30 days (90 days in Alberta). When a mistake is found and confirmed, the credit file will be corrected. If, however they verify the information as accurate, it will stay in place. At that point, the only recourse a consumer has is to submit a short note into the file outlining another interpretation, or explanation, of the facts.

In all cases, the credit bureaus need to be advised in writing. When documentation such as proof of payment can be supplied, it will speed up the research that will always be done. If someone disputes a specific item in the file, they will investigate by contacting the original source for verification. If an error is found, the item is corrected or removed. Like all good news, you wish references stayed much longer – like all bad news you wish they would go away much sooner.

One of the biggest preventative steps to avoid errors is by consistently using the same name on every application, which reduces the chance of confusion with another. Variations such as Mike or Michael or Michael A. or Michael Andrew make referencing more difficult. The more common someone's last name, the wiser it is to use a full first and middle name. Errors do happen sometimes.

Reporting companies obtain information from bankruptcy registers, court records and collection agencies. Often these files are referenced by only a debtor's name and address. It is rare that this includes birth dates or social insurance numbers, which leaves a much larger room for error when this is added to a report. It is the reason incorrect information is almost always of a negative nature when it is mistakenly shown in someone's file.

Information in credit files is generally retained for six years.

Items in credit files stay on record for various lengths of time. These parameters are as follows:

- Inquiry by a creditor – three years from the date.

- Employer and address – are updated with each inquiry.

- Secured loans – delete after a maximum six years from date file (reported).

- Judgments – purge six years from the date filed.

- Collections – both paid and unpaid stay six years from the date of last activity supplied. If there is none supplied, then five years from the assignment.

- Trade items – reports or ratings on loans or accounts drop six years from the date of last activity.

- Credit cards – always updated as a credit card continues to stay active. Missed payments showing a past due record will drop within six years of the transaction.

- Bankruptcy – six years after the date of discharge.

- O.P.D. – debt repayment programs will purge after six years from filing or three years from completion or discharge.

Credit Problems and Repairs

The most important point to understand is that no outside agency can repair someone's credit rating. They cannot fix it, change it or make credit problems disappear. Ads with these promises prey on consumers in the hope of somehow turning back the clock. They are almost always based in the United States and operate on a fee for service basis. Money up front for promises to change or update a credit rating. These firms market their services through two approaches. The first is to suggest that a written notation be placed in the credit file. It is something any consumer can do without charge by simply contacting the credit bureaus. The second avenue is advising consumers to flood agencies and the lender with dispute letters and calls. This is another approach that will have no effect. So it is almost always just the money up front part that happens. As Equifax Canada states: "Our mandate under the terms of provincial legislation includes a commitment to protection of the credit industry by assiduously maintaining file integrity."

The only guaranteed 'fix' for credit repairs is time and a consistent payment of other bills on time—every time.

From time-to-time, a certain portion of the population experience credit problems for one reason or another. The main area of concern revolves around the issue of how severe the problem really is or was. Missing one payment each year on a credit card is vastly different from having a repossession, bankruptcy or write off. Those three are the most serious credit defaults. Any of these will prevent borrowing for some time to come. Yes, mitigating circumstances do matter, but not in the case of these defaults. The reason or explanation for these is of very little interest to a lender. Their view is that a creditor did not get paid back – either on time or ever in those circumstances.

Many people have a story that they believe is totally accurate about a cousin's friend or someone else. Without fail, these stories almost always revolve around this person, after serious credit default, immediately getting some kind of unsecured credit again. Things are never as simple as they appear or there would be very little reason for anyone to repay their debts. In fact, why would anyone pay their loans if it they would just go away and another obtained without hassle?

Just as speeding tickets and at-fault accidents have a repercussion in higher insurance rates, so does previous bad credit. This is an accepted fact by anyone with a driver's license and automobile.

Only an extended period of time with no tickets or accidents mitigates a driving record. The same holds true when it comes to credit. After all, lenders rely on making a profit on each account and fully expect to be paid back on time. To make sure they know as much information as is possible, they rely on credit bureau reports for a full picture of all past credit references – good and bad.

Any bad credit reference affects credit ratings to some degree, just as a minor speeding ticket is treated differently than a major moving infraction. This causes a chain reaction, which can prevent or restrict future borrowing. In the worst cases, after seven years at most, the reference is deleted entirely. Another strong motivation to maintain a clean report is that a majority of employers use it as part of their employment verifications. Financial behaviour is part of what an employer may consider for many positions.

One day after your due-date your credit card is in arrears, with an effect on your credit rating.

What are Credit References?

Perhaps equally important is an understanding of what is not recognized as a credit reference. This list includes utilities, phone, rent and student loans. Also not accepted are references from cellular phone carriers, self-financed car lots, lay-away, payday lenders, private arrangements with doctors or simple bank overdrafts.

The only time these become credit references is when they are not paid and reported as collections or written off accounts. Useable credit references are only those from formal lenders. This ranges from financial institutions, retail credit card issuers, finance companies, credit card issuers or auto finance firms such as Ford Motor Credit, Chrysler Credit, etc.

Another shock for many involves having obtained a loan in the name of another individual, which is termed a conversion loan. The loan is made under the name of another person because the original applicant had significantly bad credit that did not qualify him or her to be added on the loan. This means someone else fronted the loan, and something that happens often, especially for the purchase of vehicles. No matter who is making the payments, the credit rating only goes to the person whose name appears on the documents. Not every lender discloses or explains the subtle, but huge difference between conversion and cosigning. It often becomes a rude awakening, but only two or three years later, when the process starts all over again, since no credit was rebuilt at all.

Chapter 9

Your Credit Score: It Matters a Lot

Perhaps a better name for this chapter is how do they really figure out so quickly if I'm approved? Well, this is where lenders use a numerical score on each application to make important credit decisions very accurately, quickly and in large quantities. Almost every bank, credit card issuer, vehicle finance company and lender of every kind and size purchase your credit score, called a FICO score, from the credit bureaus.

With their massive volume and rapid turn-around requirements, credit card issuers have always been the leaders in this field. Imagine thousands of credit card applications each day without using a simple credit score and guess how long it would take to receive an answer on an application?

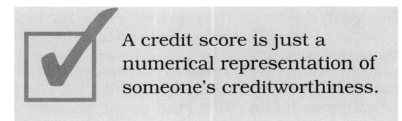

A credit score is just a numerical representation of someone's creditworthiness.

Who Cares?

If you had two friends who wanted to borrow money from you, and you knew for a statistical certainty that one would pay you back and the other might not, would you want that information before making a decision? That is the reason for your credit, or FICO score, which lenders use as one of their main, or only, tools in evaluating your credit worthiness. It was developed by the Fair Issac Company in the 1950's (hence the acronym FICO) and is software used by the credit bureaus as a uniform system.

Yes, your entire credit history is actually reduced to a three digit number ranging from the 300s to the 900. Until 2001 this score was one of the most closely guarded secrets in the credit industry. Today, it is something every person needs to know before ever starting a loan, credit card, or line of credit application, yet the vast majority of Canadians have no clue this score exists or how much it impacts their financial life.

While each lender has different criteria, a score below their internal cut-off will have lenders declining an application, or certainly charging a higher interest rate. It works and everyone uses your FICO score as a quick and accurate predictor of your credit worthiness, but it is only one of the tools. A high score simply indicates someone's level of credit risk.

Your FICO score is the key tool used to make tens of millions of credit decisions each year, as well as the determining factor of the interest rates you will be charged for many types of borrowing.

The next time you look at any application or ad, actually check the fine print to see where and how your score is used to set your rates:

• From a Visa application: "The annual interest rate is one of the following: prime + 1.9%, prime + 3.9%, prime +4.9%, prime + 5.9% or prime + 6.9% assigned by us from time to time based on an assessment of the cardholder's credit record."

• From a Dell Computers flyer: "...examples are based on 9.99%. Your monthly payments may be higher depending on your creditworthiness. Available interest rates are 9.9%, 13.9%, 16.9%, 17.9%, 18.9%, 21.9%, 26.9% and 28.9%." Depending on your credit score, your interest rates can vary by 20 percent!

• For lines of credit, this is the disclosure: "...based on the prime interest rate plus 1.9%, plus 3.9% or plus 5.9% depending on your credit record as determined in our sole discretion."

In the U.S., an applicants' credit score also establishes the interest rate on mortgages, something that will certainly be imported to Canada sooner, rather than later.

The decision made by each lender is where to place their cut-off before they will charge a higher rate or simply turn down an application. At what point will the largest number of applicants be approved without too much credit risk or collection problems down the road? Or what accounts do they say yes to, but at a higher interest rate? After all, economies of scale always dictate that any overhead costs or risks are much easier to absorb over a larger number of accounts. While the average U.S. credit score is below 700 and dropping, Canadians are still much better credit risks, with our range of scores breaking down as follows:

Below 650:	14%	651-699	11%
700-749	19%	750-799	27%
800-849	24%	850 plus:	5%

If lenders approve applications for more risky (lower score) applicants, they can get a lot more customers, but at a cost. An increase in their numbers results in more volume and more interest income. But it has to be measured against the chances of higher write-offs, bankruptcies and collection costs. It is the primary reason for the use of credit scores which really do predict losses to within a fraction of a percentage point. But even small fractions still amount to many millions of dollars for every lender.

Most people become uneasy at the thought of their credit application being handled by a computer score and not a person. Quite the opposite is true. Long gone are the days of credit personnel relying on intuition and experience. Any credit officer that had recent collection problems with a roofer, for example, is unlikely to approve anyone else in that same occupation for a long time, no matter what the next one's credit rating. Previous manual systems also tended to stereotype against divorcees (of both sexes), certain occupations or lifestyles, and often against women. None of that ever enters into a scoring system.

Factors That Impact Your Score

Both negative and positive factors influence a credit score, but each can vary in importance:

Factors that will lower a credit score:

- The length of credit history: The longer the better, because it shows a stronger track record. An ideal credit history has over 20 years of information. Five years is considered short, while a credit history of two or three years is generally too little. How the account has been paid is important, but also how long it has been in existence.

- Credit dealings: The larger any previous loan, the better. The highest amount of credit reflects the amount other lenders have advanced in the past. It includes the limit on credit cards, fixed loans and other borrowing. A small $1,000 high credit will keep the credit score quite low. A score is also reduced when lenders report to the credit bureau that payments have not been made on time. They want to see that others have been paid back over time, on time, all the time.

- Number of major credit cards: Some are good, while too many cross the line. Generally any number beyond three or four starts to negatively impact a score. It also takes into account the length of time since the last account was opened – the longer they have been in existence, the longer the track record.

 Your FICO score is totally within your control—once you know how it works.

Factors that will raise a credit score:

- The payment history: Simply put: no arrears, no collections, judgments or other negative references on a file. Of course, missing a single payment is not as serious as missing them to a number of accounts. What makes it much more serious is a second or third consecutive missed payment.

• The use of credit: Higher balances, close to their limit, will lower a score, while lower balances will reflect in a higher score. Credit can be used a lot each month, but when those accounts are paid off or greatly reduced, it positively impacts a score.

When the score is calculated, the credit decision is applied very simply. The applicant is most often approved or rejected on whether a minimum cut-off has been met. While a specific score may be acceptable to one lender, it may not approve the application somewhere else. Lenders have different risk tolerances and lending objectives that reflect what they will approve or decline in an application. They do know that these scores work. A study some years ago showed a one in nine chance that a mortgage would become over 90 days past due below a certain score. When the score was one-third higher, this chance dropped to one in almost 1,300. If it were your money, wouldn't you want those better odds of being paid back?

Your FICO score involves only the information in your credit file. Negative information, such as arrears, or a judgment, will lower your score, while an up-to-date payment history and reducing your total debt will increase your score. The importance of any one factor depends on how much (or how little) information is in the file already.

While the "how-to" of calculating each score is a closely guarded secret, the following sections and weightings combine to set each score:

30% for outstanding balances: This section compares your credit limits to the amounts owing. So moving one credit card to another, or combining two accounts, does not lower your total debt and will have no affect on your score, even though it may save you some interest. For anyone with a credit card it is also unlikely that your score will ever use a zero balance. Lenders report at various times, making it is likely that your statement balance will be used in calculating the score.

15% for the length of your total credit history: Lenders and your FICO score love to see a very long history of credit. Unfortunately, this is generally a challenge for younger people or those with only recently established credit. It considers how long specific accounts have been open and the time since you last used those open accounts.

10% for any new credit applications: Are you on track to increase your debt? For this section, the scoring considers the applications for new accounts over the past year. But it does know the difference between shopping around for one particular loan or a number of different types of accounts. It also weighs how many of your accounts are new when compared to the total you already have. After all, more credit, and very recently, can often be a sign of increased debt loads down the road.

35% for your entire payment history: This includes all your past payment records which stay on file for approximately five to seven years. Of course, any arrears are a sure-fire way to rapidly reduce your score, as will any judgment or collection. But as was discussed already, a missed credit card payment three years ago will not have the same affect as two months arrears on your vehicle payment last year. The older the information, especially when new and positive ratings are in place, the less important it is. That means your entire history is taken into account, and any old problems that you may have forgotten are still impacting your score until they are dropped entirely. What matters today, and moves your score, is to make your payments on time – every time.

10% for the types of credit you have: What is the mix of credit you are using? Are you relying only on credit cards, or is it a combination of a personal loan, cards and a vehicle payment? While it is a small factor in your score, it may not be a good idea to have open credit accounts that you don't need or use.

For anyone with a long credit history, closing an extra credit card, or paying off an account, will generally have a positive impact on their score. For someone with a shorter credit history, it may be wise to keep the longest running account open since it also has the longest track record.

One major credit card with a good limit, paid over many years, creates one of the best credit scores possible.

Even knowing a score today may not necessarily help next month, since it constantly changes and evolves as creditors report new updates. A general rule of thumb is that a score above 720 should give you the preferred, or advertised, interest rates, while a lower score will generally be charged more and it is likely that scores below 600 would not be approved under any circumstances.

Sometimes knowing the score also raises more questions than it answers. There is no printed scoring sheet, which would just show you that a new credit card lowers your score by a certain number of points. But you will always have an idea if you're making progress with your score, or taking a step backwards by increasing the number of accounts, taking on additional payments, or missing a statement date. Whatever steps you take to make some progress in increasing your score, your efforts will take 60 or 90 days to show up. It will always take that long to pay off some bills or to reduce accounts, before this information filters itself through to the credit bureaus.

Credit scoring is validated and here to stay. The original three C's of credit were character, capacity and collateral. All of these are gone today and have evolved into the new three C's of credit: computers, credit bureaus and your credit score.

Chapter 10

Budget Stuff

 A budget cannot become a straitjacket or "to the penny" rule book. It should be a game plan to celebrate, not a reason for fights.

Let's be honest. Perhaps one person in a hundred does a budget and actually follows it –and odds are you're not that person. The vast majority of people feel they work hard for their money and want the freedom to spend some of it without feeling guilty or accounting for every dime. This is not a book about budgeting – although there are many excellent sources available. Unfortunately, they can become tedious or use unrealistic examples. Yes, anyone that cuts out one latte a day could save thousands over the years, but that money never shows up, does it? Maybe skipping the lattes just makes it possible to buy some lottery tickets Friday night.

So instead of a budget would it be better to call it a Financial Reality Check and just do it every six months? The choice is yours and either option is fine. As long as you do something to set a game plan and are able to measure progress in specific ways – it's worth the effort. How much energy would you spend on getting a raise? Well, having a critical look at your expenses and your budget is even more profitable, because any raise also causes more taxes but only a small amount of extra income. That same effort in reducing interest, fees and expenses pays off in much bigger ways – for a lot more money.

Nobody can have a plan of where to go if they have no idea where they're at right now. Vagueness will not do it, so force yourself to be specific. That means it has to be in writing and include everything, especially those once a year bills like car insurance, property taxes, school fees and the like. You require a game plan for these annual bills as well. They are not a surprise, so be ready. Doing a budget cannot be done over dinner or while watching TV. It will take a little time, thought and effort over at least a week or two. Then, just like following a diet, you will need the discipline to follow it through and the results will be awesome.

Some form of budget and writing down a full list of debts is often the hardest step for many. It shows a black and white written acknowledgement of reality. It points out where all that income is really going and how little is left at the end of the day. That's the reason to get mad at yourself – to change it around, getting back in control and taking charge of your money instead of the other way around. You also have to believe in yourself, that you can do it, and that anything is possible.

The only way to achieve concrete results, little by little is to always have a game plan. It applies to budgeting just as much as financial success in life after debt. The common denominators include:

- specifics and details

- always be in writing

- include a concrete time-line for getting it done

- know your game-plan for achieving your goals

- stick to your plan – no matter what

- keep focused on your budget plan every day – don't lose sight of the goal line

A budget or financial reality check makes you accountable to yourself.

And the great thing is that it's yours to do or not do – follow or ignore – any way you see fit. After all, nobody else cares as much about your money as you do. But if a Financial Reality Check twice a year is something you can live with, here are some basic points:

- Complete the budget at the back of the book just to get a handle on where your money is going. Specifics and details matter – the more you guess or leave out, the less valuable it is.

 There are many times when you say "no big deal, it's only five bucks." Added together it is a very big deal and a lot of money.

- Forget the past: Never mind figuring out how many snacks or lunches you had last month. Start fresh and give yourself an allowance for "me" money each week. If you're in a relationship, you both get your own money – plus you will have to include some extra if you have kids. It is yours for the week to spend or save as you see fit. What does it include? You have to set the rules – are groceries and gas part of this money or is that different? Your cigarettes and night out are definitely a part of the "me" money. So now you can leave your credit and debit cards at home. You have your money for the week. Anything else is now a planned expense.

When you go on a long trip you pack differently than a workday – right? This is the same – pack your wallet different for a shopping trip than a normal weekday. The rest is up to you. If you spend it all by Thursday – you will quickly be able to tell if you're serious about your debt. You can suffer the consequences for the rest of the week or get some more money out of your account – it's all up to you. There are dozens of ways to cheat. Just loading up on junk food or cigarettes while shopping for groceries instead of using the "me" money is just one great way to cheat yourself.

- Shave something off every bill: Each bill, just this month, gets reviewed with a microscope. The goal is to find some way to reduce each and every one. It is possible, but it will take a little creative thinking and probably asking some people at work, church or in your family for ideas.

 **Finding ways to reduce every bill pays off in big ways. Make it a game not a pain.**

- Do you need call display and other phone add-ons or do you just like them? The decision is yours, but it can reduce the bill if you choose. Check your service charges or package on your bank accounts. Are you paying the basic fee or a number of other charges, too? It means your package does not meet your needs and should be changed. Plus you will likely have a number of charges for using the nearest bank machine for a fee, instead of your own.

When you've set your spending money for the week, these 'convenience charges' will disappear, plus you will be adjusting your extra service charges. For most, this change alone can easily be $30 a month.

- Is your overdraft really necessary? Do you know the interest rate and charges each month? What are the service fees and interest when paying your insurance monthly instead of annually? Yes, every bill can be reduced. All of them are important – but none of those companies are entitled to any more of your money than absolutely necessary.

Is this just a waste of time? It depends on your attitude, priorities, goal and determination. The first step is to get over that 'what's the use' mentality. Your entire debt mountain may be too big to climb right now. But as you will read in the next chapter, focus on one or two of your bills only – all of a sudden that $20 or $30 saved in a number of places start to become a little more important.

 Your budget is not meant to reduce your spending one place just to add it somewhere else.

Why Bother?

Another reason for doing a budget at least once is to become aware of how much money you actually have each month. When it comes to money and debt, it is much more valuable to be a pessimist, instead of an optimist. Thinking we can handle all those payments or downplaying the spending of an extra $100 here or there is not a recipe for financial success.

We also tend to be optimistic about our finances because we continue to focus on our gross income. Yet, that isn't anywhere near the amount we actually get to deposit into our bank account after taxes, EI, CPP, and other deductions are taken right off the top! Budgeting 101, just like managing your credit, means you cannot spend what you do not earn.

A $4,000 gross income is not $4,000. Even with the smallest of withholdings, it may be around $2,600, tops. When you deduct your rent or mortgage payments, the car payment that isn't optional this month, setting aside savings of one-twelfth of your annual bills, food, utilities and other bills that aren't negotiable each month, you'll be shocked at how little money you are actually living on. And it is only that net amount left over which makes up your financial breathing room each month and separates you from serious financial stress.

Chapter 11

Dealing With Debt

If you're broke, stressed out about your financial situation, or couldn't ever afford to miss a single paycheque – welcome to the club as you're certainly not alone. It is just not something anyone really likes to admit or talk about. It's sad but true that the last thing we ever want to say out loud is that we can't afford something, isn't it?

Debt creeps up on you little by little, here and there for one reason or another. The balances get higher, the minimum payment moves up, one account gets used to cover another, the car needs repairs, the vacation is important but goes on a credit card and so on. Savings become less, RRSPs are delayed or reduced just this year, and sometimes savings are used just this once to pay some bills.

Debt is a silent killer that starts choking you, your lifestyle and your ability to maneuver. It is something most people already realize. After all, an Ipsos-Reid survey some years ago showed that over 90 percent of Canadians listed paying down debt as their top financial goal. It stops savings and starts reversing years of hard work and discipline to build them up. The minimum payments creep up without much notice until one day – maybe not for quite a while – the juggling stops working. It might be a couple of weeks off work, unexpected repair bills, taking Christmas shopping over the top, or a host of other reasons.

Then it becomes a panic, but it is often already too late. "I never saw it coming..." yes you did – perhaps you just chose to ignore it. Maybe it was optimism that things would turn out ok or that you could manage. Maybe it came about through no fault of your own with something totally outside your control. If you are honest with yourself, that is rarely the case, however. It may be fine for many years to come; it's just that every lender is making money off you except yourself. Around 30 percent off the top for taxes, to pay groceries, utilities and the likes, then pretty much turn the rest over to payments. Yes, most of it is in interest, but treading water is better than sinking. When did that become living and not just coping?

"We are likely to produce a nation of credit drunks."
— Former U.S. Senator William Proxmire

As you're reading this chapter and thinking about your personal game plan, it is important to stay aware of the impact of future interest rate changes as well. While we will not see 15 or 20 percent rates again, they will increase again from recent historic lows. How ready are you for future increases?

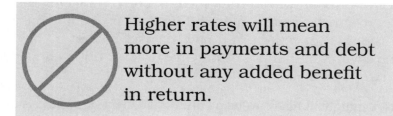

Higher rates will mean more in payments and debt without any added benefit in return.

Higher rates will not necessarily affect all your debt immediately. The mortgage may not be due for renewal yet – but it will come. Nor will credit cards readily change with each prime increase – they are high enough already. However the following will give you a good idea of the real cost of any future increases in rates. Like all bills, more interest also has to be paid with after-tax income. So for these examples, the real income needed is shown based on a 35 percent tax rate.

With only a small increase, how ready are you to spend around $500 or more on extra interest payments?

Debt amount	3% rate increase		4% rate increase	
	Before tax	After tax	Before tax	After tax
$ 15,000	$ 21	$ 32	$ 29	$ 45
$ 30,000	$ 43	$ 66	$ 58	$ 89
$ 50,000	$ 71	$109	$ 96	$148
$ 75,000	$107	$165	$143	$220
$100,000	$142	$218	$191	$294
$150,000	$214	$329	$284	$437
$200,000	$313	$482	$422	$649
$250,000	$391	$602	$528	$812

Building Financial Success

Financially successful people have no real secret. They just do what others don't want to do or find hard. They limit expenses, spend within their means, borrow only for assets that grow, not consumable debt, limit their credit card use, ask the right questions and pay themselves first by having some savings on hand. Nothing mysterious, but a challenge for many to learn.

Unfortunately, it also can be a catch-22. The largest percentage of increased consumer debt comes from those most affected by economic changes, layoffs and downsizing. Debt is increasing twice as fast for individuals earning less than $35,000 than high-income earners, plus they generally have debts with higher rates and less collateral on assets that could be sold to pay off accounts – hence the catch-22.

This is the place where we could quote a ton of statistics of what the average Canadian owes, what the average credit card balance is and so on. Unfortunately, you aren't the average. You are unique and your circumstances are unlike anyone else. Your income isn't average and neither are your challenges, specific bills, which accounts you carry, or what your own hurdles and challenges are.

Two statistics are worth knowing: 80,000 – which is the approximate number of bankruptcies a year and over $1.1 trillion, which is the total amount of debt in this country. How much of that is yours?

What's happening for many people is that things are getting worse and not better. Credit counselling agencies are now just as busy in November and December. Unusual, since almost all consumers want their credit available at least through the Christmas shopping season.

The slippery slope of excessive debt can also mean real trouble if job situations change, or often, just when overtime hours are reduced. Any slowdown in the economy will shoot up delinquency rates as consumers make priorities in their budget to pay essential bills first. Even minor changes will create higher debt loads and inability to make payments. It means more minimum payments to stall as long as possible and more arrears as those affected often use credit as a temporary bridge or substitute income.

Just like falling into a hole is easier than getting out of it – getting into debt is also much easier than turning things around. The first step is to stop adding to your debt load and to stop making things worse. According to Statistics Canada, consumer debt is rising at twice the rate of inflation and equity in our homes is actually shrinking.

No wonder when in today's cashless society it is possible to spend thousands of dollars a day and never touch any real currency. A couple of forms to purchase your stereo and no money down for a vehicle – just sign here. If that doesn't happen, there are still credit and debit cards that also contribute to piling on the debt and not a single $20 bill has physically left your pocket.

Is there Good Debt?

Is there such a thing as feeling OK about having some debts? Well, yes and no. The ultimate goal for everyone is to be debt free with a written game-plan to get there. But until that day arrives, there is such a thing as acceptable borrowing, if absolutely necessary. There is also debt that becomes more like a bad hangover after only a short time.

Acceptable borrowing or debt	Bad borrowing
An open, zero balance unsecured line of credit	'Wanna' have things
	Wedding
For a used vehicle	Furniture & appliances
To buy a house or condo	Holidays
Having one credit card	Stock market tips
For an RRSP (sometime)	For others (cosigning)
For education (within limits)	One credit card used
For a real emergency (beyond your three months' emergency savings)	to pay another
Consolidating high bills – once!	

 If you always do what you've always done then you'll always get what you've always gotten.

If you are not a homeowner, what exactly is stopping you from buying a house? For most renters it's the down payment or current debt load, right? What are you paying on finance, credit card or loan payments right now? Think of that money as standing between you and the dream of getting your own home. Without some or all of those bills you wouldn't have that cash drain and could easily save the down payment and closing costs. Get mad and get rid of them!

 **If you want anything bad enough, you'll always find a way.**

If you own a home, a mortgage is often good debt. It allowed you to purchase the house and is helping to build equity over time while the mortgage is paid off and the house increases in value. However to re-mortgage may be crossing the line of taking on bad debt. After all, the goal is to be mortgage free. If it is done to consolidate other bills, it should definitely be a one-time occurrence. It is a step backwards, so make sure the other accounts are closed and the re-mortgaged old bills are cleared as fast as possible to get back on track sooner rather than later.

Not everything in this chapter will apply to you - hopefully none of it. But if it does, you've just read the biggest lesson to learn. Get mad at yourself and start turning things around. Just like stopping a train, it will take a long time and a lot of effort and discipline. But once it's stopped – to go in a different direction will be much easier and you will never look back. Are you worth it? Are you prepared to do more of what works to get what you want – and do less of what doesn't work? Will you commit for a reason, not just a season?

Borrowing Less

It all starts with borrowing less, paying a little more and saving a little extra. Overall, there are some basic steps to review. Some of them may be obvious, but many people still aren't aware of all their options.

- Change your habits and start using a debit card instead of a credit card below a certain dollar figure.

- Can you change to a charge card (some Amex cards must be paid in full each month and have no payment options) instead of using a credit card?

- Is there a way to increase your income? Overtime, a part-time position on a temporary basis or any other options?

- Are there any savings sitting around? It might sound silly but many people carry a significant credit card balance while having a savings account or term deposit paying almost no interest.

- Is there anything you can do without?

- Can you switch to a low interest credit card, transfer your old balance to it and terminate the old card?

- Are there any assets you can sell – second car, etc?

- Are you able to move high interest debt to a line of credit?

- Where can you cut back? Lunch out every day, the daily stop for a coffee, going out to dinner less often? Every bit will help – don't minimize the impact of $10 bucks here or there. You'd be surprised how quickly it adds up.

- Can you get a bank loan against your vehicle?

After that, it will be up to you to take some steps to turn things around.

A first good step is to start treating your credit cards like writing cheques and faithfully tracking each charge. This avoids the surprise of seeing the actual total on the monthly statement. Almost everyone estimates their monthly balance too low or couldn't even name the last five things charged on their card. Sit down right now and write down what you think this month's balance will be – bet you will guess on the low side by a surprisingly large amount. When it comes to your debts, it is not the time to be overly optimistic. An American Bankers Association survey found that the typical consumer thought it would take two months to pay off Christmas shopping while their average is really around six months.

It All Starts With a Game-plan

Your budget puts things into perspective and shows where the money is going each month. Getting started on paying off your debt means having a plan of attack. Make the plan, then work the plan – no matter what. Some points that make it a little easier might be:

- Don't focus on your total debt – it's depressing and you will get that 'what's the use' feeling.

- You gave your word that you'd pay it back – keep it if at all possible. Explore all options, utilize all the resources and debt counselling tools at your disposal. When it is all said and done you will feel great that you accomplished it.

- Share your goals with others – in your family and your circle of friends – it is not a reason to be embarrassed – it's a reason to be proud. The more people that know, the more likely you are to stick with it and have a large cheering section that care about you and will support you. You won't know until you try.

- Make a plan and work the plan. Just like a budget, working the plan means discipline and sticking to it.

One thing at a time – pick your smallest bill. The one you owe the least amount of money on and tackle it first. It will create the feeling that you can do it – it will give you a sense of accomplishment and it's the smallest mountain to climb. Make your minimum payments on all the other accounts and dump everything else on the one that you have targeted. Get it set up on your web banking or through your ATM. If you skip this step you can only pay once a month when you have a statement to mail along. This will let you pay more often than just on the due dates. You want to be able to pay lots and pay often. The key is to send that extra 20 bucks when you have it. Don't put it aside hoping, wishing, and thinking it will still be around when next months' statement arrives – chances are it won't be.

Do it today – send the extra money when you can afford it. It is likely a credit card of some kind – they will take whatever you send them and post it on your account. Once a month or five times, it doesn't matter to them. You're the customer – you call the shots.

Here is what happens when making that effort on an imaginary $2,500 credit card with a 19 percent rate and three percent payments:

Making the 3% payments	Interest that month	Principal that month	New balance
$75.00	$39.58	$35.42	$2,464.58
$74.00	$39.02	$34.98	$2,429.60
skipping forward to the 24th month:			
$54.00	$28.51	$25.49	$1,775.07

Two full years and the balance is reduced by less than $700 with the minimum payments. In total, it will take close to 16 years and $2,566 in interest. Now if this payment changes to a fixed amount, where the first payment of $75 stays the same each month, it becomes:

Making the $75 payments	Interest that month	Principal that month	New balance
$75.00	$39.58	$35.42	$2,464.58
$75.00	$39.02	$35.98	$2,428.60
skipping forward to the 24th month:			
$75.00	$24.17	$50.83	$1,475.65

Here, the interest is down to $1,082 and it's done in 48 months. A full chart showing the power of an extra $20 is at the end of the book.

Could you afford to add even an extra $20 to this each

month? That will now make it $95 fixed payments and the amount toward the principal is faster and greater. It reduces the pay back to 35 months and $760 in interest. Twenty bucks will shave more than a year off the time and another $322 of interest – a huge difference, for very little extra effort.

Pick the right bill – This doesn't have to be a credit card. It can be a furniture loan or even an overdraft that is so convenient and has been on your chequing account forever. It's just that this convenience can cost you just under 20 percent interest when you use it.

- It's your call – it's your pick – Just don't kid yourself, if you're not being honest with yourself nobody else will do it for you. Since nobody else has to pay these bills and others won't care as much as you do!

 Sad but true, most people don't change until the pain level is high enough.

- Keep it in front of you – Put the last statement on the fridge or tape it to the door. It needs to always be in your face or it's out of sight – out of mind. You want that constant reminder. And every time you put any payment towards it just write it on the statement with a pen – you will actually see some progress.

- Slowly but surely – As you're no longer using this account, your statement will start looking a little weird. Instead of charges – you will have a whole lot of lines showing credits and payments and it will feel great.

- Then one day – The balance will be paid off. Chances are, if you've chosen the lowest one, it might only be a matter of months. Hey, however long it takes keep asking yourself is it worth it? You bet it is.

- It's OK to dream a little ahead of what life will be like when these bills are gone for good. What will your stress level be like? What will you be able to save for that you really want if the hangover of these bills were not around any more? Freedom is more than just being able to move around – this REAL financial freedom is just around the corner.

> You'll always find a home for that last $100 each month. Question is: will it be spent or go to savings and debt?

When the first bill is paid off, you can move on to the next. Let's assume you've found $100 in savings when you did your budget and now have a clear sense of your spending habits. Maybe you've changed the number of dinners out, started being aware of money leaking out each day and week, or perhaps just started to stretch out the length of time between drycleaners, haircuts or other discretionary spending. Just taking this $100, added to your current minimum payments, can accomplish some incredible savings.

Step-up debt repayment plan example:

1st: Department store card with $800 balance at 28%

Your minimum payment is $24 plus you are adding the $100 budget savings so will now pay $124 each month.

Was going to take: 197 months and $1,951 interest
Now paid off: in 8 months and $77 total interest

Then tackle the next one:

2nd: Credit card with $2,000 balance at 19%

The minimum payment is $60 that you've been paying while focusing on your first bill. That payment has taken the balance down to $1,784 over those eight months at $241 interest. So now you can take the $124 you were paying on the old department store card and add it to the $60 you've been paying here all along, for a total of $184.

Was going to take: 174 months and $2,007 interest
Now paid off: in 11 months and $409 total interest

3rd: Another credit card with $2,400 balance at 19%

On this balance the minimum payment is $72 which you've paid for the time while you targeting your first two bills. Now it's time to focus on this one in a serious way. Again, you're adding the $184 from above on top of the $72 you've been paying for a total of $256. As you're getting focused on this one, you've already paid that $72 for 19 months, so the balance is now $1,830 and has cost $599 in interest. But that's all about to end for this card, as well.

By now you've seen how quickly the extra payments add up. And don't forget – you've only added $100 to this, the rest is just from interest and savings by paying everybody but yourself – and it will get better.

Was going to take: 187 months and $2,454 interest
Now paid off: in another 11 months and $818 total interest

4th: Vehicle financed (student loan or other fixed loan) of $20,000 at 7%

Hurray – the last target in our example with a payment of $396. This could be your financed or leased vehicle or any other loan. While focusing on the high interest accounts for 31 months, you've reduced this balance to $10,538 and have paid $2,816 in interest to this point. Now you're adding the $396 payment to the $256 from the other bills for a total of $652.

Was going to take: 60 months and $3,763 interest
Now paid off: in another 17 months and $3,378 total interest.

The end result? You had $25,200 in debt – and were on track to pay for 15 years at a cost of more than $10,000 interest. It's taken you 47 months – less than four years - and you've saved over $5,400 interest. What has it cost you? A hundred bucks a month and a little determination!

Yes you might get a little side tracked for a month or so, but that shouldn't discourage you. It might be hard at the start, but you will quickly become a believer when you see these bills no longer showing up in the mail. Your game plan will be different, but just as powerful and satisfying. To obtain your personal breakdown, timeline, interest and savings chart, just complete the basic information at the back of the book – it will become a powerful and sure-fire roadmap for your financial success.

But it can get even better if you want. By now you've taught yourself to take charge of your money instead of giving control to all your lenders and credit card companies. You have $652 that you were paying to everybody but yourself for the last four years. If you haven't been putting some additional savings aside, this is the perfect time to start. Actually it won't be hard at all since you have the $652 available with no excuses and even better – no more bills to pay.

You saw what four years accomplished by paying others. As you will read in the next chapter, "isn't it time to pay yourself first?" This $652 each month, even at seven percent, will now grow to almost $36,000. That will be your money and not paid to any creditors. From over $25,000 in bills to debt-free in four years, and that same length of time again to create $36,000 in savings. What a difference - and it all started with a $100 off your budget each month.

By now you've seen the power of what a little extra money can do when you get rid of it right away to pay it immediately onto your balance. If you've actually stopped all or most of your charging, the balance is already lower than when you started.

Two other points to keep in mind are:

- Don't go backwards – cancel the paid-out accounts, reduce the credit limit, instruct them to discontinue allowing cash advances (see credit card chapter for the how-to's) and do whatever it takes not to have to go through this stress again.

- Can you transfer things around? Do you have a line of credit that has room to use for paying down a credit card that you've picked? It shuffles your debt around but may move it from the 17 or 19 percent range down to seven or eight percent. After all, reducing your interest is the same as saving money.

 Don't cash RRSPs to pay off debt. It jeopardizes your retirement savings and will be fully taxable when redeemed.

If you are able to move your debt to a lower rate, here is an example of what can happen with just a $2,000 balance at 18 percent versus a line of credit even at eight percent:

	Credit card paying the minimum	Credit card paying fixed payment	Line of credit paying the minimum	Line of credit paying fixed payment
1st Payment	$60.00		$60.00	
Time to pay	166 months		114 months	
Interest total	$1799		$521	
Fixed payments		$60.00		$60.00
Time to pay		47 months		38 months
Interest total		$793		$269

From here on, always ask yourself first whether you are using credit for something that is appreciating (increasing) in value or depreciating (stereo, furniture, etc.) or whether it is a consumable (such as a meal or gas).

Even a smart debt can quickly turn dumb. A $3,000 charge on your credit card can be smart if it is paid off in a month. Then the $3,000 has cost $48 in interest. If you choose to make the minimum payments each month, this $3,000 can now turn to a 17-year loan and cost you $6,124 in total!

 Make sure your credit charges are not trading a good today for a bad tomorrow.

Bad Debt Traps

The definition of debt insanity is doing the same thing you've always done and expecting different results in the future – it won't happen. You will have to do different things to have different results. Throughout this book were many tips, tools and tricks to reduce your interest or borrow smarter and shortcuts to saving interest. Here are some of them again:

1. Close but not all – Paying close to the full balance on a credit card, but not the full statement balance. It means interest is charged on the full amount of the last month – not the left over amount after you've paid a lump sum.

2. Not reducing your term on any borrowing by even just a few months when you can afford a slightly higher payment.

3. Hurray! – A credit card limit increase. More temptation for little reason and less opportunity to pay off the monthly statement if you ever do charge anywhere near the limit.

4. Carrying more than one or two cards. Quantity is not the solution as it just spreads the debts around. It generates interest profit for more lenders while often causing you

to lose track of what the totals really add up to.

5. Not having a low interest credit card when you KNOW you're going to carry a balance each month.

6. Cash advances from credit cards.

7. No payment for X months. Delaying the start of payments also delays the final payment, adds extra interest, and is often done without a good reason.

8. Making minimum payments only.

9. Considering only the price of something versus the total pay back of what it will cost when all is said and done.

10. Choosing poor priorities by not paying the highest interest debt first no matter what the balance.

11. Seven year car loans (or five year and a balloon payment)

12. Any financing longer than the reasonable or useful life of the purchase (i.e. two year vacation loan)

13. Not wanting to say I can't afford it to others or yourself.

14. Kidding yourself in the difference between gotta have and wanna have – sales and good deals are like trains – there will always be another one along very soon.

15. Forgetting or ignoring that every time a credit card is used, line of credit accessed or loan is signed that today's gain is always tomorrow's pain. What you're doing today will cost you something else you won't be able to do down the road.

16. Debt without something tangible: A car in the driveway with payments is quite different than a credit card balance with nothing left to show for it.

17. Feeling fortunate just to be approved instead of taking control, shopping around and asking questions to borrow your way and on your terms.

18. Pretending your credit card or credit line is an emergency savings account.

19. Just this one time, it will be ok if I charge...

20. Shopping around and actually buying on the same day when it's something expensive.

Chapter 12

SMART: Life after Debt

 To be financially successful you just need to do some things others won't do.

There are many different kinds of smart. The first one you've been reading and learning about throughout this book. By now you've found a number of tips and ways to save you money in concrete and measurable ways. Perhaps your SMART means Strong Motivation And the Right Tools to turn things around. Part of that is also to continue asking the right questions – sometimes the hard questions.

One of the most generous and popular savings tools for Canadians continues to be RRSPs. These retirement savings plans should be an integral part of your financial game-plan, yet less than 35 percent of individuals actually contribute and their average saving is less than $2,500. Contributions create a tax deduction and the interest earned within the RRSP keeps growing tax-free. Unlike other savings, this interest is sheltered from tax as long as it remains in the RRSP. It also creates a tax deduction in the year of the contribution. If you earned $35,000 and contributed $2,000 to your RRSP, you will pay tax on only $33,000. Since this tax has been deducted all year long on the full pay, it will create a tax refund as well.

Keep in mind that this refund is not free money. All it is doing is giving you back your own money. In a tax bracket of 30 percent, that $2,000 you've invested in yourself earns a $600 refund. This $2,000 over the next 20 years, with just an eight percent return, grows to over $9,854 without doing anything else. What a great win-win. Savings for yourself, paying less tax and getting a refund. Now if you were to do this each year for 20 years, this investment would be over $104,000. Until you reach the day of being debt-free, the smartest thing to do with any tax refund is to sign the back of the cheque and pay down one of your credit cards. If that is done, another $115 is saved in interest just over the first year. THAT is a great example of financial smarts – from beginning to end.

In 2009 the federal government also introduced a tax-free savings account (TFSA) of $5,000 a year. Unlike RRSPs, which allow contributions tax free but charge tax when they are withdrawn, TFSAs are mirrored on the U.S. style ROTH IRAs where your contributions are made with after-tax money. It may be $5,000 maximum a year, but all withdrawals are now tax-free, you can re-contribute any withdrawals, and unused contribution room is carried forward forever.

Another SMART acronym stands for Saving Money and Reducing Taxes. Let's face it, saving money also includes borrowing smarter, perhaps borrowing less, or just less frequently. It also allows you to become debt free much sooner than would otherwise be possible. The other part - saving taxes is simply another piece of your overall finance, debt and savings plan. It is another integral part of your financial jigsaw puzzle that will save you – and make you money.

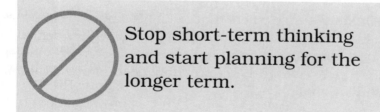

Stop short-term thinking and start planning for the longer term.

It is actually an acronym of Primerica Financial Services and may be another piece of putting together the puzzle of your financial health. Primerica's mission statement includes being "in the business of changing people's lives by helping Canadians become debt free." It also encompasses their strong desire to teach clients and empower them to make better-informed decisions with a knowledge how money, credit, insurance and investments work. What a perfect ending to this book, or perhaps a perfect beginning.

Backed by more than $1.5 trillion of assets from their parent company, Primerica is one of the fastest growing companies in the financial service field, expanding rapidly throughout the world.

Each office is an independent financial service operation with a complete range of services from mutual funds to insurance and mortgage options. Where Primerica excels head and shoulders above others is their personal dedication and service, one client at a time. What sets them apart is the training, belief and actions that the client comes first, on their terms, with their priorities, on their schedule, each with unique financial means and priorities. Or as it is sometimes referred to: "Solving the fundamental problems that keep families from reaching their goals and living their dreams."

Quite a difference from being pitched – to being helped in concrete and meaningful ways. While they don't say it – it clearly shows that each of their more than 8,000 Canadian representatives know they will only succeed when you do. They are there whether your goal is to gain an understanding of investment and insurance options, becoming debt free or starting a focused savings game plan – something big or often quite small.

It is refreshing to see a firm that talks AND practices putting the customer first. After all, wouldn't we all rather deal with someone that speaks our language, uses words and explanations we can understand and has probably been in our situation with similar challenges?

One of the unique features of Primerica's review of your financial challenges and goals is their Financial Needs Analysis. There is never any cost for this, where other firms charge upwards of $200. It is designed to walk you through specific financial, debt, insurance and savings steps to determine your needs, status and financial goals. Another excellent tool is their 45-page booklet "How Money Works" which is available from their offices. Today, portions of their materials are widely used in economic and business courses from high schools to universities – so there has to be something to it.

No matter what approach you choose or what you choose to focus on, there are some important factors to consider:

- Having a proper game plan

  It warrants pointing out again and again that a game plan must be both written and specific. That is why having a budget, or financial reality check, is an important step in the process of becoming debt-free. Is it helpful to ask for directions when you're lost in a strange city? You bet – but is it not more important to know where you are right now? Directions without knowing where you are won't help. The same is true for any game plan without first seeing the full picture of your current situation.

- Learning to take charge of your money

  It involves hard work and dedication to get back into the driver's seat. Turn your financial situation around so you control your money instead of your bills controlling you.

 **Savings prepare you for an emergency while investments help to achieve your long-term goals. Both are an invaluable part of your financial picture.**

- Starting to pay yourself first

  Granted, putting yourself first will not be easy. But when did you become less important than your bills? When did savings become a dream instead of a necessity? Do you remember your last raise? While it may not have changed your net pay much after more taxes were deducted, chances are you have now adjusted to that increased pay haven't you? Are you still barely making it at the end of the month? So where did this extra money go? Did it change your lifestyle at all? Not likely – perhaps it just went into making more payments on your debts? Well, what if that money had just been taken out of your cheque and you'd never seen it? Would you really have missed it? That's what it's like when you adopt the habit of paying yourself first. It is a difficult first step, but it will be worth it and just like the example above, you will be able to do it without much adjustment.

To start, take your savings account off your bank card access. It prevents you from using it without a plan and could also save you a lot of service charges.

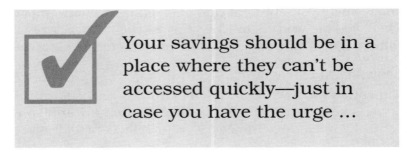

Your savings should be in a place where they can't be accessed quickly—just in case you have the urge …

- Invest and deal with a professional manager

A well-managed portfolio goes hand-in-hand with an investment relationship with someone that cares. It should be a person or company with whom you are comfortable and someone that you trust to give you options, not a sales pitch. Only then will you allow them to hold you accountable on your shared goals, allow them to ask the right questions and make your savings strategy a reality.

Directly, or indirectly, for more than one million Canadians that professional manager is AGF. The company manages more than 50 mutual funds, tailored investment programs, RSP loans and mortgages, dealing with more than 20,000 investment advisors and companies ranging from Primerica to brokerage firms.

Canadian-owned, and with a 50-year track record, AGF has in excess of $54 billion in assets under management and almost 80 percent of their mutual fund assets are ranked above the industry's median performance.

AGF also focuses a significant amount of time and talent on education, webcasts, podcasts and presentations from their top fund managers, always available at agf.com. If knowledge is power, and paying yourself first becomes an integral part of your financial success, AGF could be a great avenue and source of help. Because, without a savings game-plan, in the words of their slogan: What are you doing after work?

Another source of information is through a credit-counselling agency. A complete contact list is at the end of the book. These are professionals that will review your financial situation in strict confidence and without obligation. There is never any shame in asking for help – ever. A credit counsellor can always recommend a number of alternatives for any unique debt situation and can assist with:

- Arranging repayment schedules and terms that consumers can afford and that creditors (usually) accept.
- Developing a budget strategy that is practical and effective.
- Supplying overall credit counselling on management of debt and personal finances.
- Assisting with dispute resolution involving creditors.
- Consult and advising on (but not handle) bankruptcy procedures when necessary.

A final way to become smarter is to continue to educate yourself. Reading this book is a big step already, so give yourself full acknowledgment for it. Learning more of what works and the tools available can also mean attending a debt counselling session. It might be a trip to the library, or just doing your homework before pulling the trigger on your next purchase. Perhaps you will learn through a meeting with a personal banker at your financial institution or a range of other options. You just need to look for them, as it is often just a matter of asking.

Through these and other ways, many Canadians find assistance or a financial coach. It all starts with you, what you want to accomplish, and where you wish to be some years from now. In the words of Primerica's founder, Art Williams:

"You must develop a winning attitude." This means staying motivated for as long as it takes to have what you want.

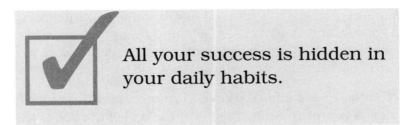

All your success is hidden in your daily habits.

Sometime tonight, take a few minutes away from interruptions if you're single. Or if you're in a relationship, grab your partner and spend some time together talking about what life will be like when you're debt free. You first have to see the goal and payoff to do the hard work necessary to get there.

Not what it could or might be like – stay focused and say what it WILL be like. What are your financial dreams or goals that you've never even thought possible?

I know you will make it happen and continue to use some of the tools to get credit smarter and get rid of debt soon. To assist you further, there are also many additional tools, calculators and resources available on a web-site designed specifically for you through: www.yourmoneybook.com

To your financial success!

George J. Boelcke, CCP
E-mail: george@vantageseminars.com
Web-site: www.yourmoneybook.com

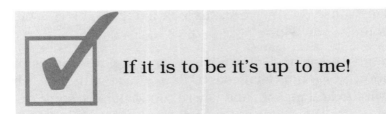

If it is to be it's up to me!

Definitions

Amortization: The repayment of a loan in regular installments of principal and interest

Amortization period: The length of time it takes to fully pay off a loan or mortgage and the total number of years over which the mortgage is set up and calculated

Appraised value: The value of an item (usually house) that is being used as collateral for a loan or mortgage and done by a professional to give an unbiased value on the item or property

Asset: What you own or can call upon such as bonds, stock, coin collections, your vehicle, house, furniture, computer, etc.

APR: Annual percentage rate - the interest rate of a loan

Balloon payment: The outstanding, unpaid amount owing at a specific point in the future, usually the lump sum required to be paid at the end of a term

Bank rate: The rate of interest charged by the Bank of Canada to chartered banks only

Behaviour scoring: A system measuring ongoing transactions of an account from the credit grantors internal systems

Base loan rate: The lowest rate based on which loans are calculated, generally, but not in all cases, being prime rate

CMHC: Canada Mortgage and Housing Corporation, a federal government agency responsible for providing assistance to consumers by insuring mortgages for lenders

Buyout: The optional purchase amount or balance owing on a lease at the end of the term

Capitalized cost: Leasing jargon for the price of the vehicle

Collateral: Any item(s) of security pledged against repayment

Collateral mortgage: A loan that is secured by a promissory note with the security of a mortgage

Conditional sales contract: A sales finance agreement against a particular item pledged for security against a regular repayment plan

Conventional mortgage: A mortgage less than 75 percent of the appraised value or of the purchase price (whichever is less)

Credit limit: The maximum amount that can be owed or outstanding on an account

Credit scoring: A system of mathematical probabilities assigned to a credit application to determine the likeliness of future repayment or collection problems

Down payment: An amount paid up front to reduce the amount of the balance to be financed

Equity: The difference when the value of something is deducted from what is owed against the asset

FICO: The acronym for Fair Isaac Company, developers of the most commonly used credit scoring model

First mortgage: The loan against a house which has first claim to the property in the event of default

Fixed rate: A charged rate of interest that does not vary during the entire duration of the loan or mortgage

Floating rate: When the interest rate charged on the loan or mortgage is adjustable (see variable rate)

Grace period: The interest free period for credit card charges of the current month

Gross Debt Service: GDS is the percentage of income per year before tax that is needed to cover payments for housing, including mortgage payments, taxes and a portion of condominium fees where applicable

High ratio mortgage: One where the amount is in excess of 75 percent of the appraised value (and thus is required to be insured by CMHC)

Installment loan: A sum advanced in exchange for fixed regular payments, normally monthly

Liability: What you owe – your debts

Marginal tax rate: The rate of tax on the last $100 of income. Income tax percentages progressively increase with earnings. This calculates the tax rate on the last (highest) amount

Maturity date: The date the loan or mortgage is due. In cases of loans it will generally be the date the debt is paid in full. For mortgages, it is also the date it needs to be re-negotiated for a further term, paid in full or transferred to a different lender

Mortgage: A loan against real property such as a house, condo or land, which then becomes the security of the loan

Mortgage broker: A specialist in mortgages whose primary function is to bring together the borrower with the lender. They are often ex-bankers or realtors and are compensated by a fee

Mortgagee: The lender of a mortgage

Mortgage renewal: The extension of a mortgage with the same lender for a further period with different terms, interest etc. that can be negotiated at the time

Mortgagor: The borrower or debtor owing the mortgage

OAC: On Approved Credit. The fine print of ads making credit offers that will only apply if someone is actually approved

Overdraft: The amount by which a withdrawal brings the balance of an account below zero on any account

PIT: Principal, Interest and taxes – of mortgage payments

Pre-payment privileges: The options of a mortgage stating how much extra can be paid and at what times during the term

Principal balance: The outstanding dollar amount of the debt

Prime rate: That interest rate charged to their most creditworthy customers by a chartered bank

Residual: The optional purchase amount or balance owing on a lease at the end of the term – generally called the buyout

Second mortgage: A further mortgage on a property when one already exists which takes second priority only over the first mortgage in the event of default and/or foreclosure

Secured loan: A loan guaranteed by security of assets pledged against repayment

Security: See collateral

Subprime: The lending category of someone with a lower or poor credit rating at high interest rates

Term: The period of time during which a loan is repaid and the agreed to interest rate is in effect. In the case of mortgages, the term may not totally repay the outstanding amount as the amortization period is a longer period of time

Unsecured loan: A loan obtained without pledging of security or assets of the borrower, also known as note loan

Variable rate: A rate of interest subject to change during the term of a loan or mortgage, usually based on a pre-agreed formula such as a certain percentage above prime

Variable rate mortgage: A mortgage where the interest rate changes (based on the prime rate) usually monthly. Mortgage payments remain the same for a period of time, but the amount that is applied to principal will vary as the interest amount will come out of the total payment first

Statement of Assets & Liabilities

	Assets	**Liabilities**	
Cash and savings	$_____	Car loan(s)	$_____
Value of current home	$_____	Bank loan(s)	$_____
Other real estate owned	$_____	Current mortgage	$_____
Stocks or bonds	$_____	Other mortgage	$_____
Cash value		Credit card balances	
of life insurance	$_____	a)_____	$_____
Automobile(s)	$_____	b)_____	$_____
	$_____	c)_____	$_____
Other assets (detail)		d)_____	$_____
_____	$_____	Other loans or debts	
_____	$_____ _____	$_____	
_____	$_____ _____	$_____	
Total assets:	$_____	**Total liabilities:**	$_____

Total assets minus total liabilities = Net worth: $_____

Debt Service and Income Calculator

Gross monthly income (before tax) $_____

Spouse monthly income (before tax) $_____

Other income (verifiable) $_____

Total Gross income: $_____

Multiply times 0.32 equals maximum

monthly mortgage payment $_____(a)

Multiply times 0.4 equals maximum

    total debt load you can carry per month $_____

Debt Load Calculation

Current monthly payments

Car loan(s) $_____

Credit card(s) minimum payment(s) $_____

Other installment plan payment(s) $_____

Other payment $_____

Other payment $_____

Total current monthly payments $_____

Available for mortgage payments:

    40% of gross income from above $_____

    Less total current monthly payments $_____

    Maximum payment available after debts $_____(b)

The maximum allowable mortgage payment is the lower figure of (a) which is 32% of your total gross income or (b) 40% of your gross income after servicing current debt.

MONTHLY SPENDING

How much spent each month: **Could you lower it by:**

HOUSING

Mortgage or rent _____

Property tax _____

Water/sewer _____

Gas _____

Electricity _____

Telephone _____

Cell phone & internet _____

Cable & satellite _____

House repairs/maintenance _____

VEHICLES & TRANSPORT

Loan or lease payment _____

Repairs/maintenance _____

Parking _____

Gas _____

Bus or train _____

FOOD

Groceries _____

Meals out _____

Lunch at work _____

CLOTHING

Adults _____

Kid(s) _____

KID'S EXPENSES

School fees & charges _____

Daycare _____

Allowance _____

Sports & other activities _____

School lunches _____

Child support payments _____

MONTHLY SPENDING
(Continued)

	How much spent each month:	Could you lower it by:

CURRENT PAYMENTS

Credit card

Credit card

Credit card

Student loan

Credit line

PERSONAL EXPENSES

Memberships

Dues & subscriptions

Presents

Personal spending money

Hairdresser

Drycleaning

PAYING YOURSELF

RRSP monthly savings

Other savings plan

INSURANCE

Vehicle

House or content

Life

Disability

MEDICAL

Prescriptions

Dental

Eye care

Drugs/vitamins

ENTERTAINMENT

Sports & recreation

GRAND TOTAL:

$:	$:
TOTAL SPENT EACH MONTH	**TOTAL POSSIBLE SAVINGS**

Mortgage Homework Check-list

Before setting out to find your mortgage, here is a partial list of questions and paperwork to get ready in order to pre-qualify:

1. Income worksheet completed   ____

2. Debt calculation sheet completed   ____

3. Net worth/asset sheet completed   ____

Copies of:

4. Proof of income last two years
   (preferably the Federal Government Notice of
   Assessment or T-4s or the first page of the last
   two tax returns to show your gross income.   ____

5. A letter from your employer confirming length
   of employment, gross income and whether you
   are full-time permanent, part time, etc.   ____

6. Your most recent pay stub from this year, which
   should show the income year-to-date.   ____

7. Receipts for any loans, credit cards or other bills
   you have paid in full over the past couple of months
   as they will not yet be off your credit bureau report
   when the lender calculates your debt load to see if
   you can afford the mortgage payments.   ____

8. The completed and signed offer to purchase
   if you have already found the house you wish to buy.   ____

9. The name of the lawyer to use for the
   mortgage documentation and disbursement of funds.   ____

10. Proof of down payment – where it is from.
    Your lender needs to verify that you have the money
    for the down payment and it is not also borrowed.
    A copy of your passbook, term deposit or
    bank machine slip to verify the balance.   ____

11. Before the mortgage starts, I will pay off these bills to lower my debt load: _____

_____

12. I have savings for our other closing costs (about 1.5 percent of the total purchase price) _____

I want the mortgage to be:

Open_____ Closed_____

For a total amortization of _____ years

And a term of _____ years (before needing to renew.)

I/we want our property taxes added to our mortgage payments___ paid on our own each year____

I/we want our mortgage payments to be calculated and made:

Monthly___ Semi-monthly___ Bi-monthly___ Weekly___ (where available with the lender of your choice)

I have $_____ down payment available, which is 20 percent or more of the purchase price___(for a conventional mortgage) or less than 20 percent so it will add CMHC insurance on a high ratio mortgage_____

Promissory Note (example only)

Date:_____

FOR VALUE RECEIVED, I,_____,

(name of borrower)

in the City of _____, Province of_____,

hereby promise to pay to the order of _____,

(name of lender)

the sum of _____($_____) dollars

(spell out the amount)

with interest at the rate of ___% per annum as follows:

Date Payable   Amount Payable

1)_____

2)_____

3)_____

4)_____

5)_____

6)_____

Presentment for payment, demand, protest and notice of dishonour are hereby waived and the endorser hereby agrees to remain as fully liable as if every presentment, protest and notice hereby waived were fully made and given.

_____   _____

(Witness signature)   (Signature of borrower)

This is not a legal document, but only an example of a possible agreement.
Always consult a professional for specific legal and contract advice.

Contact Information

Selected Provincial Credit Counselling Agencies

Alberta
Credit Counselling Services of Alberta
225 -602-11 Ave SW
Calgary, AB T2R 1J8   888 294 0076

British Columbia
Credit Counselling Society of British Columbia
330-435 Columbia St
New Westminster, BC V3L 5N8   888 527 8999

Manitoba
Community Financial Counselling Services
3rd floor – 238 Portage Ave
Winnipeg, MB R3C 0B1   888 573 2383

Newfoundland
Credit Counselling Service of Atlantic Canada
22 Queens Rd
St. John's, NF A1C 2A5   709 753 5812

New Brunswick
Credit Counselling Services of Atlantic Canada
133 Prince William St., #703
Saint John, NB E2L 2B5   888 753 2227

Nova Scotia
Credit Counselling Service of Atlantic Canada
6080 Young St., #1003
Halifax, NS B3K 5L2   888 753 2227

Ontario
Ontario Association of Credit Counselling Services – Main contact
Box 189
Grimsby, ON L3M 4G3   905 945 5644

Prince Edward Island
Credit Counselling Services of Atlantic Canada
342 Grafton St., #203
Charlottetown, PEI C1A 1L8   888 753 2227

Saskatchewan
Provincial Mediation Board – Credit Counselling
120 - 2151 Scarth St.
Regina, SK S4P 3V7   888 215 2222

Schedule I Banks in Canada

BMO Bank of Montreal
First Canadian Place
Box 1
Toronto, ON M5X 1A1
www.bmo.com   416 867 5000

ScotiaBank (The Bank of Nova Scotia)
Scotia Plaza
7th Floor, 40 King Street W
Toronto, ON M5H 1H1
www.scotiabank.ca   416 866 6161

CIBC
Commerce Court West
56th Floor – 199 Bay Street
Toronto, ON M5L 1A2
www.cibc.com   416 980   2211

Canadian Western Bank
2300-10303 Jasper Ave
Edmonton, AB T5J 3X6
www.cwbank.com   780 423 8888

Laurentian Bank of Canada
1981 McGill College Ave.
Montreal, PQ H3A 3K3
www.laurentianbank.com   514 522 1846

National Bank of Canada
4th Floor – 600 de La Gauchetiere Street W
Montreal, PQ H3L 4L2
www.nbc.ca   514 394 4000

RBC (Royal Bank of Canada)
8th Floor - 200 Bay Street
Toronto, ON M5J 2J5
www.royalbank.com   416 974 5151

TD Bank Financial Group (includes Canada Trust)
P.O. Box 1
Toronto Dominion Centre
Toronto, ON M5K 1A2
www.td.com   866 222 3456

For all bank contact information, check the website of the Canadian Bankers' Association at cba.ca

Credit Unions

Selected Provincial Contacts & Information:

British Columbia (49 credit unions with 368 locations
                & 1,629,000 members)
     Credit Union Central of BC
     Telephone: 604 734 2511
     Web-site: www.cucbc.com

Alberta (48 credit unions with 211 locations & 644,000 members)
     Credit Union Central Alberta Ltd.
     Telephone: 403 258 5900
     Web-site: www.albertacentral.com

Saskatchewan (75 credit unions with 314 locations & 525,000 members)
Sask Central
Telephone: 866 403 7499
Web-site: www.saskcu.com

Manitoba (57 credit unions with 208 locations & 589,000 members)
Credit Union Central of Manitoba
Telephone: 204 985 4700
Web-site: creditunion.mb.ca

Ontario (195 credit unions with 652 locations & 1,603,000 members)
Credit Union Central of Ontario
Telephone: 905 238 9400
Web-site: www.ontariocreditunions.com

New Brunswick (52 credit unions with 125 locations & 285,000 members)
Telephone: 506 857 8184
Web-site: www.creditunion.nb.ca

Nova Scotia (33 credit unions with 82 locations & 169,000 members)
Credit Union Central of Nova Scotia
Telephone: 902 453 0680
Web-site: www.ns-credit-unions.com

Prince Edward Island (10 credit unions with 15 locations
& 64,000 members)
Telephone: 902 566 3350
Web-site: www.peicreditunions.com

Credit Bureaus Contacts

Equifax Canada – Consumer Relations
Box 190, Jean Talon Station
Montreal, PQ H1S 2Z2
Toll-free: 800 465 7166
Fax: 514 355 8502
Web-site: www.equifax.ca

Trans Union Canada
Box 338, LCD 1
Hamilton, ON L8L 7W2
Toll-free: 800 663 9980
Fax: 905 527 0401
Web-site: www.tcu.ca

Northern Credit Bureaus
336 Rideau Blvd.
Rouyn-Noranda, PQ J9X 1P2
Web-site: www.creditbureau.ca

Principal Issuers of
Visa and MasterCard in Canada:

Visa:

Bank of America
Bank of Nova Scotia
Caisses Populaires Desjardins
CIBC
Citizens Bank of Canada
Home Trust
Laurentian Bank
Royal Bank
TD Bank (with Canada Trust)
US Bank
Vancouver City Savings Credit Union

MasterCard:

Alberta Treasury Branch
Bank of Montreal
Canadian Tire Acceptance Ltd.
Capital One
Citibank Canada
Credit Union Electronic Transaction Services
G.E. Capital Corp.
MBNA Canada
National Bank of Canada
President's Choice Financial
Wells Fargo/Trans Canada
Sears Canada

Reference Tables & Charts

Credit Card Payments
13% rate - making minimum 3% payment
Or: Add $20 and make fixed payments

Card balance	Minimum payments	Months to pay in full	Total interest	Add $20 and fix payments	Months to pay in full	Total interest now	Interest saved
$ 500	$ 15	63	$ 177	$ 35	16	$ 46	$ 131
$ 750	$22.5	84	$ 318	$42.5	20	$ 87	$ 231
$ 1,000	$ 30	99	$ 459	$ 50	23	$ 133	$ 326
$ 1,500	$ 45	120	$ 742	$ 65	27	$ 235	$ 507
$ 2,000	$ 60	135	$1,024	$ 80	30	$ 345	$ 679
$ 2,500	$ 75	146	$1,307	$ 95	32	$ 459	$ 848
$ 3,000	$ 90	156	$1,590	$ 110	33	$ 575	$1,015
$ 3,500	$ 105	164	$1,872	$ 125	34	$ 693	$1,179
$ 4,000	$ 120	170	$2,155	$ 140	35	$ 812	$1,343
$ 4,500	$ 135	177	$2,437	$ 155	36	$ 932	$1,505
$ 5,000	$ 150	182	$2,720	$ 170	36	$1,053	$1,667
$ 6,000	$ 180	191	$3,285	$ 200	37	$1,296	$1,989
$ 7,000	$ 210	199	$3,850	$ 230	38	$1,539	$2,311
$ 8,000	$ 240	206	$4,416	$ 260	38	$1,784	$2,632
$ 9,000	$ 270	212	$4,981	$ 290	39	$2,029	$2,952
$10,000	$ 300	218	$5,546	$ 320	39	$2,275	$3,271

Credit Card Payments
19% rate - making minimum 3% payment
Or: Add $20 and make fixed payments

Card balance	Minimum payments	Months to pay in full	Total interest	Add $20 and fix payments	Months to pay in full	Total interest now	Interest saved
$ 500	$ 15	77	$ 330	$ 35	17	$ 71	$ 259
$ 750	$22.5	105	$ 610	$42.5	21	$ 136	$ 474
$ 1,000	$ 30	125	$ 889	$ 50	25	$ 212	$ 677
$ 1,500	$ 45	154	$ 1,448	$ 65	29	$ 382	$1,066
$ 2,000	$ 60	174	$ 2,007	$ 80	30	$ 522	$1,485
$ 2,500	$ 75	189	$ 2,566	$ 95	35	$ 760	$1,806
$ 3,000	$ 90	202	$ 3,124	$ 110	36	$ 958	$2,166
$ 3,500	$ 105	213	$ 3,683	$ 125	38	$1,161	$2,522
$ 4,000	$ 120	222	$ 4,242	$ 140	39	$1,367	$2,875
$ 4,500	$ 135	231	$ 4,801	$ 155	40	$1,574	$3,227
$ 5,000	$ 150	238	$ 5,360	$ 170	40	$1,783	$3,577
$ 6,000	$ 180	251	$ 6,477	$ 200	42	$2,203	$4,274
$ 7,000	$ 210	262	$ 7,595	$ 230	42	$2,627	$4,968
$ 8,000	$ 240	271	$ 8,712	$ 260	43	$3,053	$5,659
$ 9,000	$ 270	279	$ 9,830	$ 290	44	$3,480	$6,350
$10,000	$ 300	287	$10,948	$ 320	44	$3,909	$7,039

Credit Card Payments

28% rate - making minimum 3% payment
Or: Add $20 and make fixed payments

Card balance	Minimum payments	Months to pay in full	Total interest	Add $20 and fix payments	Months to pay in full	Total interest now	Interest saved
$ 500	$ 15	126	$ 902	$ 35	18	$ 115	$ 787
$ 750	$22.5	187	$ 1,777	$42.5	24	$ 228	$ 1,549
$1,000	$ 30	230	$ 2,652	$ 50	28	$ 363	$ 2,289
$1,500	$ 45	291	$ 4,402	$ 65	34	$ 679	$ 3,723
$2,000	$ 60	334	$ 6,152	$ 80	38	$1,036	$ 5,116
$2,500	$ 75	367	$ 7,902	$ 95	42	$1,421	$ 6,481
$3,000	$ 90	394	$ 9,651	$ 110	44	$1,824	$ 7,827
$3,500	$ 105	417	$11,401	$ 125	46	$2,241	$ 9,160
$4,000	$ 120	437	$13,151	$ 140	48	$2,669	$10,482
$4,500	$ 135	455	$14,901	$ 155	50	$3,103	$11,798
$5,000	$ 150	471	$16,651	$ 170	51	$3,544	$13,107
$6,000	$ 180	498	$20,151	$ 200	53	$4,440	$15,711

Low Credit Card Rate Comparisons

Card Issuer	Minimum limit	APR	Grace period	Fees	Rewards program
BMO Bank of Montreal					Air miles or
Mosaik MC low rate option	?	11.4	19	$35	cash back
Mosaik MC/Air Miles	?	11.4	19	$70	Air miles
CIBC					
Select Visa Card	500	11.5	21	$29	
Citizens Bank					
Shared Interest Visa	500	11.25	21	$50	Various
Coast Capital Savings					
Low rate Coast Visa	500	11.4	21	$25	Bonus $
HSBC					
Low rate MC	500	12.9	23	$25	
Low rate MC with rewards	500	12.9	23	$60	Various
Laurentian Bank					
Black Visa reduced rate	500	11.49	21	$25	
National Bank					
Reduced rate MC	1000	14.5	21	$45	Points
Reduced rate Ultramar MC	500	14.5	21	$15	Rebates
Reduced rate Escapade MC	1000	14.5	21	$35	Points
Syncro MC	500	Pr+4 or 6	21	$35	
Royal Bank					
Classic Visa low rate	1000	11.5	21	$20	
Scotiabank					
Value Visa	1000	13.9	26	$ 0	
No fee Value Visa	1000	11.4	26	$29	
ScotiaLine Visa	10 000	Pr+2-7	26	$ 0	
TD Canada Trust					
Emerald Visa	1000	Pr+1.9-6.9	21+	$25	
VanCity Credit Union					
Envirofund Visa low interest	500	11.25	21	$25	
Classic My Visa	500	11.25	21	$50	Points

Standard Credit Card Rate Comparisons

Card Issuer	Minimum limit	APR	Grace period	Fees	Rewards program
Amex Bank					
Holt Renfrew card	1000	18.99	21	$ 0	Holt Renfrew points
No Fee Air miles	1000	18.5	21	$ 0	Air miles
BMO Bank of Montreal					
Mosaik MC no fee option	?	18.5	19	$ 0	Air miles/CB
Canadian Tire					
Options MC	300	10.99-25.99	21+	$ 0	Can Tire money
CIBC					
Classic Aero Visa	500	19.5	21	$29	Aeroplan miles
Classic Visa	500	18.5	21	$ 0	
Dividend Card	500	19.5	21	$ 0	to 1% cash back
Shoppers Visa	500	19.5	21	$ 0	Shoppers points
Citibank					
Citi Drivers' Edge MC	750	19.9	21-25	$ 0	cash back
Citi Enrich MC	750	19.9	21-25	$ 0	cash back/cars
Citi MasterCard	750	18.5	21-25	$ 0	
Petro Points MC	750	19.9	21-25	$ 0	discounts
Coast Capital Savings					
Coast Capital Visa	500	18.4	21	$ 0	Bonus $
CUETS Financial					
CUETS Low fee MC	1000	19.49	21	$24	Choice rewards
Low fee MC	1000	19.5	21	$12	
HSBC					
HSBC MC	500	22.9	21	$59	
MC with Rewards	500	22.9	21	$59	points
JP Morgan Chase					
Chase MC	500	18.99	21	$ 0	
Sears MC	500	18.9	21	$ 0	Sears points
Laurentian Bank					
Black Visa	500	19.49	21	$ 0	

Standard Credit Card Rate Comparisons - cont'd

Card Issuer	Minimum limit	APR	Grace period	Fees	Rewards program
MBNA					
Preferred MC	500	17.99	25	$ 0	
National Bank					
Escapade MC	1000	19.5	21	$20	Points toward merch.
Husky/Mohawk MC	1000	19.5	21	$ 0	1% cash back
Regular MC	500	19.5	21	$ 0	
Sunoco MC	500	19.9	21	$ 0	
Ultramar MC	500	19.9	21	$ 0	Cash back Ultramar
President's Choice Bank					
Financial MC	1000	19.9-24	21	$ 0	grocery cash back
Royal Bank					
Esso Visa	1000	19.5	21	$ 0	Points/Esso
Mike Weir Visa	1000	19.5	21	$35	Points
RBC Rewards Visa	1000	19.5	21	$ 0	Points
Starbucks Visa	1000	19.5	21	$ 0	Duetto $
Visa Classic	1000	18.5	21	$ 0	
Visa Classic II	1000	19.5	21	$35	Travel or RBC points
Scotiabank					
Classic Money Back Visa	1000	18.5	26	$ 8	Up to 1% cash back
No fee Money Back Visa	1000	19.5	26	$ 0	Up to 1% cash back
Scene Visa	1000	19.5	26	$ 0	Movie points
TD Canada Trust					
Green Visa	500	19.75	21+	$ 0	
GM Card	500	19.75	21+	$ 0	3% cash back toward car
Rebate Rewards Visa	500	19.75	21	$ 0	Tiered CA back
VanCity Credit Union					
Envirofund Visa	500	17.75	21	$ 0	
Silver Visa	500	17.75	21	$39	Points towards merch.

Retail Credit Card Rate Comparisons

Card Issuer	Minimum limit	APR	Grace period	Fees	Rewards program
HBC (GE Money) HBC Credit Card	300	28.8	25	$ 0	HBC rewards
Sears (JP Morgan) Sears Card	300	28.8	25	$ 0	Reward options
Wal Mart (GE Money) Wal Mart Visa	500	28.8	25	$ 0	

Secured Credit Card Rate Comparisons

Card Issuer	Minimum limit	APR	Grace period	Fees	Deposit & rewards
Capital One Bank Secured MC	300	PR+13.55	25	$59	75-300
Home Trust Secured Visa	1000	24.99	21	$90-$120	as credit limit
Peoples Trust Horizon Secured MC	500	19.5	25	$5.95/M	same as credit limit
Van City Credit Union Secured MC	500	19.5	21	$0	500

Low-rate Student Credit Card Rate Comparisons

Card Issuer	Minimum limit	APR	Grace period	Fees	Rewards program
BMO Bank of Montreal Student Mosaik MC/Westjet	?	11.4	19	$25	Air Miles
Student Mosaik MC/Cash back	?	11.4	19	$84	Cash back
Student Mosaik MC/No fee	?	11.4	19	$ 0	You select
Student Mosaik MC/Air Miles	?	11.4	19	$70	Air Miles
Coast Capital Savings Coast Student Visa	300	11.4	21	$25	
Desjardins Low interest Visa	300	11.4	21	$25	
Westminster Cr. Union Low interest Visa	300	11.4	21	$25	

Selected Regular-Rate Gold Cards

Card Issuer	Minimum limit	APR	Grace period	Fees	Rewards program
Amex Bank					
Air Miles Gold	1000	18.5	21	$0	air miles
BMO Bank of Montreal					
Westjet MC	?	18.5	18	$90	air miles
Capital One Bank					
Gold MC	500	Pr+14	25	$59	
CIBC					
CIBC Aerogold	5000	19.5	21	$120	aeroplan miles
Gold Visa	5000	19.5	21	$99	points
Citibank Canada					
Citi Gold MC	750	18.5	21+	$0	
Coast Capital Savings					
Coast Visa	5000	19.9	21	$0	bonus dollars
CUETS Financial					
CUETS Gold MC	5000	19.49	21	$96	
HSBC Bank					
HSBC Gold MC	500	19.9	21	$60	
MBNA Canada					
Gold MC	2500	17.99	25	$0	
Royal Bank					
RBC Reward Visa	5000	19.5	21	$90	points
Visa Gold	5000	19.5	21	$0	
Scotiabank					
No fee Gold Visa	5000	19.5	26	$0	
TD/Canada Trust					
TD Gold Select	5000	19.75	21+	$0	
TD Gold Travel	5000	19.75	21+	$120	travel points
Vancity Credit Union					
Enviro Gold Visa	5000	19.5	21	99	points

Credit Card Service & Transaction Fees

Selecting a credit card also involves selecting the right combination of fees and charges. Depending on your use of the card, these can add up to substantial additional costs. It is also important to first read and understand the specific terms and conditions of any card.

Card Issuer	Cash Advance Fee plus convenience fee*	Over the limit fee	Foreign currency conversion fee
Amex Bank	$2.75	$20	2.2% – 2.5%
BMO Bank of Montreal	$1.50 – $4.00	$25	2.5%
Canadian Tire	$4.00	$ 0	2.5%
Capital One	1% Min $5, max. $10	$20	2.5%
CIBC	$2.50	$20	2.5%
Citibank	$3.00	$20	2.5%
Citizens Bank	$2.00	$10	2%
Coast Capital Savings	$1.25	$ 0	1.8%
CUETS Financial	$2.00	$10	2.5%
Home Trust	$2.00	$29	2.0%
HSBC Bank	$2.00-$3.00	$29	2.5%
JP Morgan Chase	$3.00-no max.	$10-$25	2.5%
Laurentian Bank	$2.25	$ 0	2.5%
MBNA Canada	1% Min $7.50	$35	2.5%
National Bank	$2 – $2.50	$ 0	2.5%
President's Choice	0 – $2.50	$20	2.5%
Royal Bank	$2.50	$20	2.5%
Scotiabank	$2.00	$20	2.5%
TD Canada Trust	$2.00	$20	2.5%
Vancity Credit Union	$2.00	$10	2%
Westminster Savings	$1.25	$ 0	1.8%

* Convenience fees are additional fees charged by so called white label machines, or an ATM not owned by the financial institution whose account you are accessing.

Source of credit card comparison information & service fees: Financial Consumer Agency of Canada

Finance Payment Tables

Term in Years

$	Rate	2.0	3.0	3.5	4.0	4.5	5.0
$1,000	6.0%	$44	$30	$26	$23	$21	$19
	6.5%	$45	$31	$27	$24	$21	$20
	7.0%	$45	$31	$27	$24	$22	$20
	7.5%	$45	$31	$27	$24	$22	$20
	8.0%	$45	$31	$27	$24	$22	$20
	8.5%	$45	$32	$28	$25	$22	$21
	9.0%	$46	$32	$28	$25	$23	$21
	9.5%	$46	$32	$28	$25	$23	$21
	10.0%	$46	$32	$28	$25	$23	$21
	10.5%	$46	$33	$29	$26	$23	$21
	11.0%	$47	$33	$29	$26	$24	$22
$2,000	6.0%	$89	$61	$53	$47	$42	$39
	6.5%	$89	$61	$53	$47	$43	$39
	7.0%	$90	$62	$54	$48	$43	$40
	7.5%	$90	$62	$54	$48	$44	$40
	8.0%	$90	$63	$55	$49	$44	$41
	8.5%	$91	$63	$55	$49	$45	$41
	9.0%	$91	$64	$56	$50	$45	$42
	9.5%	$92	$64	$56	$50	$46	$42
	10.0%	$92	$65	$57	$51	$46	$42
	10.5%	$93	$65	$57	$51	$47	$43
	11.0%	$93	$65	$58	$52	$47	$43
$3,000	6.0%	$133	$91	$79	$70	$64	$58
	6.5%	$134	$92	$80	$71	$64	$59
	7.0%	$134	$93	$81	$72	$65	$59
	7.5%	$135	$93	$81	$73	$66	$60
	8.0%	$136	$94	$82	$73	$66	$61
	8.5%	$136	$95	$83	$74	$67	$62
	9.0%	$137	$95	$84	$75	$68	$62
	9.5%	$138	$96	$84	$75	$68	$63
	10.0%	$138	$97	$85	$76	$69	$64
	10.5%	$139	$98	$86	$77	$70	$64
	11.0%	$140	$98	$86	$78	$71	$65
$4,000	6.0%	$177	$122	$106	$94	$85	$77
	6.5%	$178	$123	$107	$95	$86	$78
	7.0%	$179	$124	$108	$96	$87	$79
	7.5%	$180	$124	$109	$97	$88	$80
	8.0%	$181	$125	$110	$98	$88	$81
	8.5%	$182	$126	$110	$99	$89	$82
	9.0%	$183	$127	$111	$100	$90	$83
	9.5%	$184	$128	$111	$100	$91	$84
	10.0%	$185	$129	$113	$101	$92	$85
	10.5%	$186	$130	$114	$102	$93	$86
	11.0%	$186	$131	$115	$103	$94	$87

Term in Years

$	Rate	2.0	3.0	3.5	4.0	4.5	5.0
$5,000	6.0%	$222	$152	$132	$117	$106	$97
	6.5%	$223	$153	$133	$119	$107	$98
	7.0%	$224	$154	$135	$120	$108	$99
	7.5%	$225	$156	$136	$121	$109	$100
	8.0%	$226	$157	$137	$122	$111	$101
	8.5%	$227	$158	$138	$123	$112	$103
	9.0%	$228	$159	$139	$124	$113	$104
	9.5%	$230	$160	$140	$126	$114	$105
	10.0%	$231	$161	$142	$127	$115	$106
	10.5%	$232	$163	$143	$128	$117	$107
	11.0%	$233	$164	$144	$129	$118	$109
$6,000	6.0%	$266	$183	$159	$141	$127	$116
	6.5%	$267	$184	$160	$142	$128	$117
	7.0%	$269	$185	$161	$144	$130	$119
	7.5%	$270	$187	$163	$145	$131	$120
	8.0%	$271	$188	$164	$146	$133	$122
	8.5%	$273	$189	$166	$148	$134	$123
	9.0%	$274	$191	$167	$149	$136	$125
	9.5%	$275	$192	$168	$151	$137	$126
	10.0%	$277	$194	$170	$152	$138	$127
	10.5%	$278	$195	$171	$153	$140	$129
	11.0%	$280	$196	$173	$155	$141	$130
$7,000	6.0%	$310	$213	$185	$164	$148	$135
	6.5%	$323	$215	$187	$166	$450	$137
	7.0%	$313	$216	$188	$168	$151	$139
	7.5%	$315	$218	$190	$169	$153	$140
	8.0%	$317	$219	$192	$171	$155	$142
	8.5%	$318	$221	$193	$173	$156	$144
	9.0%	$320	$223	$195	$174	$158	$145
	9.5%	$321	$224	$197	$176	$160	$147
	10.0%	$323	$226	$198	$178	$162	$149
	10.5%	$325	$228	$200	$179	$163	$150
	11.0%	$326	$229	$202	$181	$165	$152
$8,000	6.0%	$355	$243	$212	$188	$169	$155
	6.5%	$356	$245	$213	$190	$171	$157
	7.0%	$358	$247	$215	$192	$173	$158
	7.5%	$360	$249	$217	$193	$175	$160
	8.0%	$362	$251	$219	$195	$177	$162
	8.5%	$364	$253	$221	$197	$179	$164
	9.0%	$365	$254	$223	$199	$181	$166
	9.5%	$367	$256	$225	$201	$183	$168
	10.0%	$367	$258	$227	$203	$185	$170
	10.5%	$371	$260	$228	$206	$187	$172
	11.0%	$373	$262	$230	$207	$188	$174

Term in Years

$	Rate	2.0	3.0	3.5	4.0	4.5	5.0
$9,000	6.0%	$399	$274	$238	$211	$191	$174
	6.5%	$401	$276	$240	$213	$193	$176
	7.0%	$403	$278	$242	$216	$195	$178
	7.5%	$405	$280	$244	$218	$197	$180
	8.0%	$407	$282	$246	$220	$199	$182
	8.5%	$409	$284	$248	$222	$201	$185
	9.0%	$411	$286	$251	$224	$203	$187
	9.5%	$413	$288	$253	$226	$205	$189
	10.0%	$415	$290	$255	$228	$208	$191
	10.5%	$417	$293	$257	$230	$210	$193
	11.0%	$419	$295	$259	$233	$212	$196
$10,000	6.0%	$443	$304	$265	$235	$211	$193
	6.5%	$445	$306	$267	$237	$214	$196
	7.0%	$448	$309	$269	$239	$216	$198
	7.5%	$450	$311	$271	$242	$219	$200
	8.0%	$452	$313	$274	$244	$221	$203
	8.5%	$455	$316	$276	$246	$224	$205
	9.0%	$457	$318	$278	$249	$226	$208
	9.5%	$459	$320	$281	$251	$228	$210
	10.0%	$461	$323	$283	$254	$231	$212
	10.5%	$464	$325	$286	$256	$233	$215
	11.0%	$466	$327	$288	$258	$236	$217
$11,000	6.0%	$488	$335	$291	$258	$233	$213
	6.5%	$490	$337	$294	$261	$235	$215
	7.0%	$493	$340	$296	$263	$238	$218
	7.5%	$495	$342	$299	$266	$241	$220
	8.0%	$498	$345	$301	$269	$243	$223
	8.5%	$500	$347	$304	$271	$246	$226
	9.0%	$503	$350	$306	$274	$248	$228
	9.5%	$505	$352	$309	$276	$251	$231
	10.0%	$508	$355	$311	$279	$254	$234
	10.5%	$510	$358	$314	$282	$256	$236
	11.0%	$513	$360	$317	$284	$259	$239
$12,000	6.0%	$532	$365	$317	$282	$254	$232
	6.5%	$535	$368	$320	$285	$257	$235
	7.0%	$537	$371	$323	$287	$260	$238
	7.5%	$540	$373	$326	$290	$263	$240
	8.0%	$543	$376	$329	$293	$265	$243
	8.5%	$545	$379	$331	$296	$268	$246
	9.0%	$548	$382	$334	$299	$271	$249
	9.5%	$551	$384	$337	$301	$274	$252
	10.0%	$554	$387	$340	$304	$277	$255
	10.5%	$557	$390	$343	$307	$280	$258
	11.0%	$559	$393	$346	$310	$283	$261

Term in Years

$	Rate	2.0	3.0	3.5	4.0	4.5	5.0
$13,000	6.0%	$576	$395	$344	$305	$275	$251
	6.5%	$579	$398	$347	$308	$278	$254
	7.0%	$582	$401	$350	$311	$281	$257
	7.5%	$585	$404	$353	$314	$284	$260
	8.0%	$588	$407	$356	$317	$287	$264
	8.5%	$591	$410	$359	$320	$291	$267
	9.0%	$594	$413	$362	$324	$294	$270
	9.5%	$597	$416	$365	$327	$298	$273
	10.0%	$600	$419	$368	$330	$300	$276
	10.5%	$603	$423	$371	$333	$303	$279
	11.0%	$606	$426	$374	$336	$306	$283
$14,000	6.0%	$620	$426	$370	$329	$296	$270
	6.5%	$624	$429	$373	$332	$300	$274
	7.0%	$627	$432	$377	$335	$303	$277
	7.5%	$630	$435	$380	$339	$306	$281
	8.0%	$633	$439	$383	$342	$310	$284
	8.5%	$636	$442	$387	$345	$313	$287
	9.0%	$640	$445	$390	$348	$316	$291
	9.5%	$643	$448	$393	$352	$320	$294
	10.0%	$646	$452	$396	$355	$323	$297
	10.5%	$649	$455	$340	$358	$326	$301
	11.0%	$653	$458	$403	$362	$330	$304
$15,000	6.0%	$665	$456	$397	$352	$318	$290
	6.5%	$668	$460	$400	$356	$321	$293
	7.0%	$672	$463	$404	$359	$325	$297
	7.5%	$675	$467	$407	$363	$328	$301
	8.0%	$678	$470	$411	$366	$332	$304
	8.5%	$682	$474	$414	$370	$335	$308
	9.0%	$685	$477	$418	$373	$339	$311
	9.5%	$689	$480	$421	$377	$342	$315
	10.0%	$692	$484	$425	$380	$346	$319
	10.5%	$696	$488	$428	$384	$350	$322
	11.0%	$699	$491	$432	$388	$352	$326
$16,000	6.0%	$709	$487	$423	$376	$339	$309
	6.5%	$713	$490	$427	$379	$343	$313
	7.0%	$716	$494	$431	$383	$346	$317
	7.5%	$720	$498	$434	$387	$350	$321
	8.0%	$724	$501	$438	$391	$354	$324
	8.5%	$727	$505	$442	$394	$358	$328
	9.0%	$731	$509	$446	$398	$361	$332
	9.5%	$735	$513	$449	$402	$365	$336
	10.0%	$738	$516	$453	$406	$369	$340
	10.5%	$742	$520	$457	$410	$373	$343
	11.0%	$746	$524	$460	$414	$377	$348

Term in Years

$	Rate	2.0	3.0	3.5	4.0	4.5	5.0
$17,000	**6.0%**	$753	$517	$450	$399	$360	$329
	6.5%	$757	$521	$454	$403	$364	$333
	7.0%	$761	$525	$458	$407	$368	$337
	7.5%	$765	$529	$461	$411	$372	$341
	8.0%	$769	$533	$465	$415	$376	$345
	8.5%	$773	$537	$469	$419	$380	$349
	9.0%	$777	$541	$473	$423	$384	$353
	9.5%	$781	$545	$477	$427	$388	$357
	10.0%	$784	$549	$481	$431	$392	$361
	10.5%	$788	$553	$485	$435	$396	$365
	11.0%	$792	$557	$490	$439	$401	$370
$18,000	**6.0%**	$798	$548	$476	$423	$381	$348
	6.5%	$802	$552	$480	$427	$385	$352
	7.0%	$806	$556	$484	$431	$390	$356
	7.5%	$810	$560	$489	$435	$394	$361
	8.0%	$814	$564	$493	$439	$398	$365
	8.5%	$818	$568	$497	$444	$402	$369
	9.0%	$822	$572	$501	$448	$407	$374
	9.5%	$824	$577	$505	$452	$411	$378
	10.0%	$831	$581	$510	$457	$415	$382
	10.5%	$835	$585	$514	$461	$420	$387
	11.0%	$839	$589	$518	$462	$424	$391
$19,000	**6.0%**	$842	$578	$503	$446	$402	$367
	6.5%	$846	$582	$507	$451	$407	$372
	7.0%	$851	$587	$511	$455	$411	$376
	7.5%	$855	$591	$516	$459	$416	$381
	8.0%	$859	$595	$520	$464	$420	$385
	8.5%	$864	$600	$525	$468	$425	$390
	9.0%	$868	$601	$529	$473	$429	$394
	9.5%	$872	$609	$534	$477	$434	$399
	10.0%	$877	$613	$538	$482	$438	$403
	10.5%	$881	$618	$543	$486	$443	$408
	11.0%	$886	$622	$547	$491	$448	$413
$20,000	**6.0%**	$886	$608	$529	$470	$424	$387
	6.5%	$891	$613	$534	$474	$428	$391
	7.0%	$895	$618	$538	$479	$433	$396
	7.5%	$900	$622	$543	$484	$438	$401
	8.0%	$905	$627	$548	$488	$442	$406
	8.5%	$909	$631	$552	$493	$447	$410
	9.0%	$914	$636	$557	$498	$452	$415
	9.5%	$918	$641	$562	$502	$457	$420
	10.0%	$923	$645	$566	$507	$461	$425
	10.5%	$928	$650	$571	$512	$466	$430
	11.0%	$932	$655	$576	$517	$471	$435

Term in Years

$	Rate	2.0	3.0	3.5	4.0	4.5	5.0
$21,000	6.0%	$931	$639	$556	$493	$445	$406
	6.5%	$935	$644	$560	$498	$450	$411
	7.0%	$940	$648	$565	$503	$454	$416
	7.5%	$945	$653	$570	$508	$459	$421
	8.0%	$950	$658	$575	$513	$464	$426
	8.5%	$955	$663	$580	$518	$469	$431
	9.0%	$959	$668	$585	$523	$474	$436
	9.5%	$964	$673	$590	$528	$479	$441
	10.0%	$969	$678	$595	$533	$485	$446
	10.5%	$974	$683	$600	$538	$490	$451
	11.0%	$979	$688	$605	$543	$495	$457
$22,000	6.0%	$975	$669	$582	$517	$466	$425
	6.5%	$980	$674	$587	$522	$471	$430
	7.0%	$985	$679	$592	$527	$476	$436
	7.5%	$990	$684	$597	$532	$481	$441
	8.0%	$995	$689	$602	$537	$486	$446
	8.5%	$1,000	$694	$607	$542	$492	$451
	9.0%	$1,005	$700	$613	$547	$497	$457
	9.5%	$1,010	$705	$618	$553	$502	$462
	10.0%	$1,015	$710	$623	$558	$508	$467
	10.5%	$1,020	$715	$628	$563	$513	$473
	11.0%	$1,025	$720	$633	$569	$518	$478
$23,000	6.0%	$1,019	$700	$608	$540	$487	$445
	6.5%	$1,025	$705	$614	$545	$492	$450
	7.0%	$1,030	$710	$619	$551	$498	$455
	7.5%	$1,035	$715	$624	$556	$503	$461
	8.0%	$1,040	$721	$630	$561	$509	$466
	8.5%	$1,045	$726	$635	$567	$514	$472
	9.0%	$1,051	$731	$640	$572	$520	$477
	9.5%	$1,056	$737	$646	$578	$525	$483
	10.0%	$1,061	$742	$651	$583	$531	$489
	10.5%	$1,067	$748	$657	$589	$536	$494
	11.0%	$1,072	$753	$662	$594	$542	$500
$24,000	6.0%	$1,064	$730	$635	$564	$508	$464
	6.5%	$1,069	$736	$640	$569	$514	$470
	7.0%	$1,075	$741	$646	$575	$519	$475
	7.5%	$1,080	$747	$651	$580	$525	$481
	8.0%	$1,085	$752	$657	$586	$531	$487
	8.5%	$1,091	$758	$663	$592	$536	$492
	9.0%	$1,096	$763	$668	$597	$542	$498
	9.5%	$1,102	$769	$674	$603	$548	$504
	10.0%	$1,107	$774	$680	$609	$554	$510
	10.5%	$1,113	$780	$685	$614	$560	$516
	11.0%	$1,119	$786	$691	$620	$565	$522

Term in Years

$	Rate	2.0	3.0	3.5	4.0	4.5	5.0
$25,000	6.0%	$1,108	$761	$661	$587	$529	$483
	6.5%	$1,114	$766	$667	$593	$535	$489
	7.0%	$1,119	$772	$673	$599	$541	$495
	7.5%	$1,125	$778	$679	$604	$547	$501
	8.0%	$1,131	$783	$684	$610	$553	$507
	8.5%	$1,136	$789	$690	$616	$559	$513
	9.0%	$1,142	$795	$696	$622	$565	$519
	9.5%	$1,148	$801	$702	$628	$571	$525
	10.0%	$1,154	$807	$708	$634	$577	$531
	10.5%	$1,159	$813	$714	$640	$583	$537
	11.0%	$1,165	$818	$720	$646	$589	$544
$26,000	6.0%	$1,152	$791	$688	$611	$551	$503
	6.5%	$1,158	$797	$694	$617	$557	$509
	7.0%	$1,164	$803	$700	$623	$563	$515
	7.5%	$1,170	$809	$706	$629	$569	$521
	8.0%	$1,176	$815	$712	$635	$575	$527
	8.5%	$1,182	$821	$718	$641	$581	$533
	9.0%	$1,188	$827	$724	$647	$587	$540
	9.5%	$1,194	$833	$730	$653	$594	$546
	10.0%	$1,200	$839	$736	$659	$600	$552
	10.5%	$1,206	$845	$742	$666	$606	$559
	11.0%	$1,212	$851	$749	$672	$613	$565
$27,000	6.0%	$1,197	$821	$714	$634	$572	$522
	6.5%	$1,203	$828	$720	$640	$578	$528
	7.0%	$1,209	$834	$727	$647	$584	$535
	7.5%	$1,215	$840	$733	$653	$591	$541
	8.0%	$1,221	$846	$739	$659	$597	$547
	8.5%	$1,227	$852	$745	$666	$603	$554
	9.0%	$1,233	$859	$752	$672	$610	$560
	9.5%	$1,240	$865	$758	$678	$616	$567
	10.0%	$1,246	$871	$765	$685	$623	$574
	10.5%	$1,252	$878	$771	$691	$630	$580
	11.0%	$1,258	$884	$777	$698	$636	$587
$28,000	6.0%	$1,241	$852	$741	$658	$593	$541
	6.5%	$1,247	$858	$747	$664	$599	$548
	7.0%	$1,254	$865	$754	$670	$606	$554
	7.5%	$1,260	$871	$760	$677	$613	$561
	8.0%	$1,266	$877	$767	$684	$619	$568
	8.5%	$1,273	$884	$773	$690	$626	$574
	9.0%	$1,279	$890	$780	$697	$633	$581
	9.5%	$1,286	$897	$786	$703	$639	$588
	10.0%	$1,292	$903	$793	$710	$646	$595
	10.5%	$1,299	$910	$800	$717	$653	$602
	11.0%	$1,305	$917	$806	$724	$660	$609

Mortgage Payment Table 4.25% Rate

Number of Years	Paying monthly	Paying semi-monthly	Paying bi-weekly	Paying weekly
1	85.25	42.59	39.31	19.64
2	43.52	21.74	20.06	10.03
3	29.62	14.80	13.65	6.82
4	22.67	11.33	10.45	5.22
5	18.51	9.25	8.53	4.27
6	15.74	7.86	7.26	3.63
7	13.77	6.88	6.35	3.17
8	12.29	6.14	5.66	2.83
9	11.14	5.57	5.13	2.57
10	10.23	5.11	4.71	2.36
11	9.48	4.74	4.37	2.18
12	8.86	4.43	4.08	2.04
13	8.34	4.16	3.84	1.92
14	7.89	3.94	3.64	1.82
15	7.50	3.75	3.46	1.73
16	7.17	3.58	3.30	1.65
17	6.87	3.43	3.17	1.58
18	6.61	3.30	3.05	1.52
19	6.38	3.19	2.94	1.47
20	6.17	3.08	2.84	1.42
21	5.99	2.99	2.76	1.38
22	5.82	2.91	2.68	1.34
23	5.66	2.83	2.61	1.30
24	5.52	2.76	2.54	1.27
25	5.40	2.70	2.49	1.24

EACH $1,000 OF MORTGAGE X FACTOR = BLENDED PAYMENT.

Mortgage Payment Table 4.00% Rate

Number of Years	Paying monthly	Paying semi-monthly	Paying bi-weekly	Paying weekly
1	85.13	42.53	39.26	19.62
2	43.41	21.69	20.02	10.00
3	29.51	14.74	13.61	6.80
4	22.56	11.27	10.40	5.20
5	18.40	9.19	8.48	4.24
6	15.63	7.81	7.21	3.60
7	13.65	6.82	6.29	3.15
8	12.17	6.08	5.61	2.80
9	11.03	5.51	5.08	2.54
10	10.11	5.05	4.66	2.33
11	9.36	4.68	4.31	2.16
12	8.74	4.37	4.03	2.01
13	8.22	4.10	3.79	1.89
14	7.77	3.88	3.58	1.79
15	7.38	3.69	3.40	1.70
16	7.04	3.52	3.25	1.62
17	6.75	3.37	3.11	1.55
18	6.48	3.24	2.99	1.49
19	6.25	3.12	2.88	1.44
20	6.04	3.02	2.78	1.39
21	5.85	2.92	2.70	1.35
22	5.68	2.84	2.62	1.31
23	5.53	2.76	2.55	1.27
24	5.39	2.69	2.48	1.24
25	5.26	2.63	2.42	1.21

Mortgage Payment Table   4.50% Rate

Number of Years	Paying monthly	Paying semi-monthly	Paying bi-weekly	Paying weekly
1	85.36	42.64	39.35	19.67
2	43.63	21.79	20.11	10.05
3	29.73	14.85	13.70	6.85
4	22.78	11.38	10.50	5.25
5	18.62	9.30	8.58	4.29
6	15.85	7.92	7.31	3.65
7	13.88	6.93	6.40	3.20
8	12.40	6.20	5.72	2.86
9	11.26	5.62	5.19	2.59
10	10.34	5.17	4.77	2.38
11	9.60	4.79	4.42	2.21
12	8.98	4.49	4.14	2.07
13	8.46	4.23	3.90	1.95
14	8.01	4.00	3.69	1.85
15	7.63	3.81	3.51	1.76
16	7.29	3.64	3.36	1.68
17	7.00	3.50	3.22	1.61
18	6.74	3.37	3.11	1.55
19	6.51	3.25	3.00	1.50
20	6.30	3.15	2.90	1.45
21	6.12	3.06	2.82	1.41
22	5.95	2.97	2.74	1.37
23	5.80	2.90	2.67	1.33
4	5.66	2.83	2.61	1.30
25	5.53	2.76	2.55	1.27

EACH $1,000 OF MORTGAGE X FACTOR = BLENDED PAYMENT.

Mortgage Payment Table   4.75% Rate

Number of Years	Paying monthly	Paying semi-monthly	Paying bi-weekly	Paying weekly
1	85.47	42.69	39.40	19.69
2	43.74	21.85	20.16	10.08
3	29.84	14.90	13.75	6.87
4	22.90	11.44	10.55	5.27
5	18.74	9.36	8.64	4.32
6	15.97	7.98	7.36	3.68
7	14.00	6.99	6.45	3.22
8	12.52	6.25	5.77	2.88
9	11.37	5.68	5.24	2.62
10	10.46	5.23	4.82	2.41
11	9.72	4.85	4.48	2.24
12	9.10	4.55	4.19	2.10
13	8.58	4.29	3.95	1.98
14	8.14	4.06	3.75	1.87
15	7.75	3.87	3.57	1.79
16	7.42	3.71	3.42	1.71
17	7.13	3.56	3.28	1.64
18	6.87	3.43	3.16	1.58
19	6.64	3.32	3.06	1.53
20	6.44	3.22	2.96	1.48
21	6.25	3.12	2.88	1.44
22	6.09	3.04	2.80	1.40
23	5.94	2.97	2.73	1.37
24	5.80	2.90	2.67	1.33
25	5.67	2.83	2.61	1.31

Mortgage Payment Table   5.25% Rate

Number of Years	Paying monthly	Paying semi-monthly	Paying bi-weekly	Paying weekly
1	85.70	42.80	39.50	19.74
2	43.96	21.96	20.26	10.13
3	30.06	15.01	13.85	6.92
4	23.12	11.55	10.65	5.32
5	18.96	9.47	8.74	4.37
6	16.19	8.09	7.46	3.73
7	14.23	7.10	6.55	3.28
8	12.75	6.37	5.88	2.94
9	11.61	5.80	5.35	2.67
10	10.70	5.34	4.93	2.46
11	9.96	4.97	4.59	2.29
12	9.35	4.67	4.31	2.15
13	8.83	4.41	4.07	2.03
14	8.39	4.19	3.86	1.93
15	8.01	4.00	3.69	1.84
16	7.68	3.84	3.54	1.77
17	7.39	3.69	3.40	1.70
18	7.14	3.56	3.29	1.64
19	6.91	3.45	3.18	1.59
20	6.71	3.35	3.09	1.54
21	6.53	3.26	3.00	1.50
22	6.36	3.18	2.93	1.46
23	6.22	3.10	2.86	1.43
24	6.08	3.04	2.80	1.40
25	5.96	2.98	2.74	1.37

EACH $1,000 OF MORTGAGE X FACTOR = BLENDED PAYMENT.

Mortgage Payment Table   5.00% Rate

Number of Years	Paying monthly	Paying semi-monthly	Paying bi-weekly	Paying weekly
1	85.58	42.75	39.45	19.72
2	43.85	21.90	20.21	10.10
3	29.95	14.96	13.80	6.90
4	23.01	11.49	10.60	5.30
5	18.85	9.41	8.69	4.34
6	16.08	8.03	7.41	3.70
7	14.11	7.05	6.50	3.25
8	12.64	6.31	5.82	2.91
9	11.49	5.74	5.30	2.65
10	10.58	5.29	4.88	2.44
11	9.84	4.91	4.53	2.27
12	9.22	4.61	4.25	2.12
13	8.70	4.35	4.01	2.00
14	8.26	4.13	3.81	1.90
15	7.88	3.94	3.63	1.81
16	7.55	3.77	3.48	1.74
17	7.26	3.63	3.34	1.67
18	7.00	3.50	3.23	1.61
19	6.77	3.38	3.12	1.56
20	6.57	3.28	3.03	1.51
21	6.39	3.19	2.94	1.47
22	6.22	3.11	2.87	1.43
23	6.07	3.03	2.80	1.40
24	5.94	2.97	2.73	1.37
25	5.82	2.91	2.68	1.34

Mortgage Payment Table   5.75% Rate

Number of Years	Paying monthly	Paying semi-monthly	Paying bi-weekly	Paying weekly
1	85.92	42.91	39.60	19.79
2	44.18	22.06	20.36	10.17
3	30.28	15.12	13.95	6.97
4	23.34	11.66	10.76	5.37
5	19.19	9.58	8.84	4.42
6	16.42	8.20	7.57	3.78
7	14.46	7.21	6.66	3.33
8	12.99	6.49	5.98	2.99
9	11.85	5.92	5.46	2.73
10	10.94	5.47	5.04	2.52
11	10.21	5.10	4.70	2.35
12	9.59	4.79	4.42	2.21
13	9.08	4.54	4.18	2.09
14	8.64	4.32	3.98	1.99
15	8.27	4.13	3.81	1.90
16	7.94	3.97	3.66	1.83
17	7.66	3.82	3.52	1.76
18	7.40	3.70	3.41	1.70
19	7.18	3.59	3.31	1.65
20	6.98	3.49	3.21	1.61
21	6.80	3.40	3.13	1.57
22	6.64	3.32	3.06	1.53
23	6.50	3.25	2.99	1.50
24	6.37	3.18	2.93	1.46
25	6.25	3.12	2.88	1.44

EACH $1,000 OF MORTGAGE X FACTOR = BLENDED PAYMENT.

Mortgage Payment Table   5.50% Rate

Number of Years	Paying monthly	Paying semi-monthly	Paying bi-weekly	Paying weekly
1	85.81	42.86	39.55	10.77
2	44.07	22.01	20.31	10.15
3	30.17	15.07	13.90	6.95
4	23.23	11.60	10.70	5.35
5	19.07	9.53	8.79	4.39
6	16.31	8.15	7.51	3.76
7	14.34	7.16	6.61	3.30
8	12.87	6.43	5.93	2.96
9	11.73	5.86	5.40	2.70
10	10.82	5.40	4.99	2.49
11	10.08	5.04	4.64	2.32
12	9.47	4.73	4.36	2.18
13	8.95	4.47	4.12	2.06
14	8.52	4.25	3.92	1.96
15	8.14	4.06	3.75	1.87
16	7.81	3.90	3.60	1.80
17	7.52	3.76	3.46	1.73
18	7.27	3.63	3.35	1.67
19	7.04	3.52	3.24	1.62
20	6.84	3.42	3.15	1.57
21	6.66	3.33	3.07	1.53
22	6.50	3.25	2.99	1.50
23	6.36	3.17	2.93	1.46
24	6.22	3.11	2.87	1.43
25	6.10	3.05	2.81	1.40

Mortgage Payment Table   6.00% Rate

Number of Years	Paying monthly	Paying semi-monthly	Paying bi-weekly	Paying weekly
1	86.03	42.96	39.65	19.81
2	44.29	22.12	20.41	10.20
3	30.39	15.18	14.00	7.00
4	23.45	11.71	10.81	5.40
5	19.30	9.64	8.89	4.44
6	16.54	8.26	7.62	3.81
7	14.57	7.28	6.71	3.35
8	13.11	6.54	6.04	3.02
9	11.97	5.98	5.51	2.76
10	11.07	5.53	5.10	2.55
11	10.33	5.16	4.76	2.38
12	9.72	4.85	4.48	2.24
13	9.21	4.60	4.24	2.12
14	8.77	4.38	4.04	2.02
15	8.40	4.19	3.87	1.93
16	8.07	4.03	3.72	1.86
17	7.79	3.89	3.59	1.79
18	7.54	3.77	3.47	1.73
19	7.32	3.65	3.37	1.68
20	7.12	3.56	3.28	1.64
21	6.95	3.47	3.20	1.60
22	6.79	3.39	3.12	1.56
23	6.64	3.32	3.06	1.53
24	6.52	3.25	3.00	1.50
25	6.40	3.20	2.94	1.47

Mortgage Payment Table   6.25% Rate

Number of Years	Paying monthly	Paying semi-monthly	Paying bi-weekly	Paying weekly
1	86.14	43.02	39.70	19.84
2	44.40	22.17	20.46	10.22
3	30.50	15.23	14.05	7.02
4	23.56	11.77	10.86	5.43
5	19.41	9.69	8.94	4.47
6	16.65	8.32	7.67	3.83
7	14.69	7.34	6.77	3.38
8	13.22	6.60	6.09	3.04
9	12.09	6.04	5.57	2.78
10	11.19	5.59	5.15	2.57
11	10.45	5.22	4.81	2.41
12	9.85	4.92	4.53	2.27
13	9.34	4.66	4.30	2.15
14	8.90	4.45	4.10	2.05
15	8.53	4.26	3.93	1.96
16	8.21	4.10	3.78	1.89
17	7.93	3.96	3.65	1.82
18	7.68	3.83	3.53	1.77
19	7.46	3.72	3.43	1.72
20	7.26	3.63	3.34	1.67
21	7.09	3.54	3.26	1.63
22	6.93	3.46	3.19	1.59
23	6.79	3.39	3.13	1.56
24	6.66	3.33	3.07	1.53
25	6.55	3.27	3.01	1.51

EACH $1,000 OF MORTGAGE X FACTOR = BLENDED PAYMENT.

Mortgage Payment Table   6.75% Rate

Number of Years	Paying monthly	Paying semi-monthly	Paying bi-weekly	Paying weekly
1	86.37	43.12	39.80	19.89
2	44.62	22.28	20.56	10.27
3	30.72	15.34	14.15	7.07
4	23.79	11.88	10.96	5.48
5	19.64	9.81	9.05	4.52
6	16.88	8.43	7.78	3.89
7	14.93	7.45	6.87	3.44
8	13.46	6.72	6.20	3.10
9	12.33	6.16	5.68	2.84
10	11.43	5.71	5.27	2.63
11	10.71	5.35	4.93	2.46
12	10.10	5.04	4.65	2.32
13	9.60	4.79	4.42	2.21
14	9.17	4.58	4.22	2.11
15	8.80	4.39	4.05	2.02
16	8.48	4.23	3.90	1.95
17	8.20	4.09	3.77	1.89
18	7.96	3.97	3.66	1.83
19	7.74	3.86	3.56	1.78
20	7.55	3.77	3.47	1.74
21	7.38	3.68	3.39	1.70
22	7.22	3.61	3.32	1.66
23	7.09	3.54	3.26	1.63
24	6.96	3.48	3.20	1.60
25	6.85	3.42	3.15	1.57

EACH $1,000 OF MORTGAGE X FACTOR = BLENDED PAYMENT.

Mortgage Payment Table   6.50% Rate

Number of Years	Paying monthly	Paying semi-monthly	Paying bi-weekly	Paying weekly
1	86.26	43.07	39.75	19.86
2	44.51	22.22	20.51	10.25
3	30.61	15.28	14.10	7.05
4	23.68	11.82	10.91	5.45
5	19.53	9.75	9.00	4.49
6	16.77	8.37	7.72	3.86
7	14.81	7.39	6.82	3.41
8	13.34	6.66	6.15	3.07
9	12.21	6.10	5.62	2.81
10	11.31	5.65	5.21	2.60
11	10.58	5.28	4.87	2.43
12	9.97	4.98	4.59	2.29
13	9.47	4.73	4.36	2.18
14	9.03	4.51	4.16	2.08
15	8.66	4.33	3.99	1.99
16	8.34	4.17	3.84	1.92
17	8.06	4.03	3.71	1.85
18	7.82	3.90	3.60	1.80
19	7.60	3.79	3.50	1.75
20	7.41	3.70	3.41	1.70
21	7.23	3.61	3.33	1.66
22	7.08	3.53	3.26	1.63
23	6.94	3.46	3.19	1.60
24	6.81	3.40	3.13	1.57
25	6.70	3.34	3.08	1.54

Mortgage Payment Table   7.00% Rate

Number of Years	Paying monthly	Paying semi-monthly	Paying bi-weekly	Paying weekly
1	86.48	43.18	39.85	19.91
2	44.73	22.33	20.61	10.30
3	30.83	15.39	14.20	7.10
4	23.90	11.93	11.01	5.50
5	19.75	9.86	9.10	4.55
6	17.00	8.49	7.83	3.91
7	15.04	7.51	6.83	3.46
8	13.58	6.78	6.26	3.13
9	12.46	6.22	5.74	2.87
10	11.56	5.77	5.32	2.66
11	10.83	5.41	4.99	2.49
12	10.23	5.11	4.71	2.35
13	9.73	4.86	4.48	2.24
14	9.30	4.64	4.28	2.14
15	8.93	4.46	4.11	2.05
16	8.62	4.30	3.97	1.98
17	8.34	4.16	3.84	1.92
18	8.10	4.04	3.73	1.86
19	7.88	3.94	3.63	1.81
20	7.69	3.84	3.54	1.77
21	7.52	3.76	3.46	1.73
22	7.37	3.68	3.39	1.70
23	7.24	3.61	3.33	1.66
24	7.11	3.55	3.27	1.64
25	7.00	3.50	3.22	1.61

EACH $1,000 OF MORTGAGE X FACTOR = BLENDED PAYMENT.

Mortgage Payment Table   7.25% Rate

Number of Years	Paying monthly	Paying semi-monthly	Paying bi-weekly	Paying weekly
1	86.59	43.23	39.90	19.94
2	44.84	23.39	20.66	10.32
3	30.94	15.45	14.25	7.12
4	24.01	11.99	11.06	5.53
5	19.87	9.92	9.15	4.57
6	17.12	8.55	7.88	3.94
7	15.16	7.57	6.98	3.49
8	13.70	6.84	6.31	3.15
9	12.58	6.28	5.79	2.89
10	11.68	5.83	5.38	2.69
11	10.96	5.47	5.05	2.52
12	10.36	5.17	4.77	2.38
13	9.86	4.92	4.54	2.27
14	9.43	4.71	4.34	2.17
15	9.07	4.53	4.17	2.09
16	8.75	4.37	4.03	2.01
17	8.48	4.23	3.90	1.95
18	8.24	4.11	3.79	1.89
19	8.03	4.01	3.69	1.85
20	7.84	3.91	3.61	1.80
21	7.67	3.83	3.53	1.76
22	7.52	3.76	3.46	1.73
23	7.39	3.69	3.40	1.70
24	7.27	3.63	3.34	1.67
25	7.16	3.57	3.29	1.65

Mortgage Payment Table 7.75% Rate

Number of Years	Paying monthly	Paying semi-monthly	Paying bi-weekly	Paying weekly
1	86.82	43.34	40.00	10.98
2	45.06	22.49	20.76	10.37
3	31.16	15.56	14.35	7.17
4	24.24	12.10	11.16	5.58
5	20.10	10.03	9.26	4.62
6	17.35	8.66	7.99	3.99
7	15.40	7.69	7.09	3.54
8	13.95	6.96	6.42	3.21
9	12.83	6.40	5.90	2.95
10	11.94	5.96	5.49	2.75
11	11.22	5.60	5.16	2.58
12	10.62	5.30	4.89	2.44
13	10.12	5.05	4.66	2.33
14	9.70	4.84	4.47	2.23
15	9.34	4.66	4.30	2.15
16	9.03	4.51	4.16	2.08
17	8.76	4.37	4.03	2.01
18	8.53	4.26	3.92	1.96
19	8.32	4.15	3.83	1.91
20	8.13	4.06	3.74	1.87
21	7.97	3.98	3.67	1.83
22	7.83	3.91	3.60	1.80
23	7.70	3.84	3.54	1.77
24	7.58	3.78	3.49	1.74
25	7.47	3.73	3.44	1.72

EACH $1,000 OF MORTGAGE X FACTOR = BLENDED PAYMENT.

Mortgage Payment Table 7.50% Rate

Number of Years	Paying monthly	Paying semi-monthly	Paying bi-weekly	Paying weekly
1	86.70	43.29	39.95	19.96
2	44.95	22.44	20.71	10.35
3	31.05	15.50	14.30	7.15
4	24.13	12.04	11.11	5.55
5	19.98	9.98	9.20	4.60
6	17.23	8.60	7.94	3.97
7	15.28	7.63	7.04	3.52
8	13.83	6.90	6.37	3.18
9	12.70	6.34	5.85	2.92
10	11.81	5.90	5.44	2.72
11	11.09	5.54	5.10	2.55
12	10.49	5.24	4.83	2.41
13	9.99	4.99	4.60	2.30
14	9.57	4.78	4.40	2.20
15	9.21	4.60	4.24	2.12
16	8.89	4.44	4.09	2.04
17	8.62	4.30	3.97	1.98
18	8.38	4.18	3.86	1.93
19	8.17	4.08	3.76	1.88
20	7.99	3.99	3.67	1.84
21	7.82	3.90	3.60	1.80
22	7.67	3.83	3.53	1.76
23	7.54	3.75	3.47	1.73
24	7.42	3.71	3.41	1.71
25	7.32	3.65	3.36	1.68

Mortgage Payment Table 8.25% Rate

Number of Years	Paying monthly	Paying semi-monthly	Paying bi-weekly	Paying weekly
1	87.04	43.45	40.09	20.03
2	45.28	22.60	20.86	10.42
3	31.39	15.67	14.46	7.22
4	24.47	12.21	11.27	5.63
5	20.33	10.15	9.36	4.68
6	17.59	8.78	8.10	4.05
7	15.64	7.81	7.20	3.60
8	14.19	7.08	6.53	3.26
9	13.08	6.53	6.02	3.01
10	12.19	6.09	5.61	2.80
11	11.48	5.73	5.28	2.64
12	10.89	5.43	5.01	2.50
13	10.39	5.19	4.78	2.39
14	9.98	4.98	4.59	2.29
15	9.62	4.80	4.43	2.21
16	9.31	4.65	4.29	2.14
17	9.05	4.52	4.16	2.08
18	8.82	4.40	4.06	2.03
19	8.61	4.30	3.96	1.98
20	8.43	4.21	3.88	1.94
21	8.27	4.13	3.81	1.90
22	8.13	4.06	3.74	1.87
23	8.01	4.00	3.68	1.84
24	7.89	3.94	3.63	1.81
25	7.79	3.89	3.58	1.79

EACH $1,000 OF MORTGAGE X FACTOR = BLENDED PAYMENT.

Mortgage Payment Table 8.00% Rate

Number of Years	Paying monthly	Paying semi-monthly	Paying bi-weekly	Paying weekly
1	86.93	43.39	40.05	20.01
2	45.17	22.55	20.81	10.39
3	31.28	15.61	14.41	7.20
4	24.35	12.16	11.21	5.60
5	20.21	10.09	9.31	4.65
6	17.47	8.72	8.04	4.02
7	15.52	7.75	7.15	3.57
8	14.07	7.02	6.48	3.24
9	12.95	6.47	5.96	2.98
10	12.06	6.02	5.55	2.77
11	11.35	5.66	5.22	2.61
12	10.75	5.37	4.95	2.47
13	10.26	5.12	4.72	2.36
14	9.84	4.91	4.53	2.26
15	9.48	4.73	4.36	2.18
16	9.17	4.58	4.22	2.11
17	8.90	4.44	4.10	2.04
18	8.67	4.33	3.99	1.99
19	8.47	4.23	3.89	1.95
20	8.28	4.14	3.81	1.90
21	8.12	4.05	3.74	1.87
22	7.98	3.98	3.67	1.83
23	7.85	3.92	3.61	1.80
24	7.74	3.86	3.56	1.78
25	7.63	3.81	3.51	1.75

Mortgage Payment Table   8.75% Rate

Number of Years	Paying monthly	Paying semi-monthly	Paying bi-weekly	Paying weekly
1	87.26	43.55	40.19	20.08
2	45.50	22.71	20.95	10.47
3	31.61	15.78	14.56	7.27
4	24.69	12.32	11.37	5.68
5	20.56	10.26	9.47	4.73
6	17.83	8.90	8.21	4.10
7	15.89	7.93	7.31	3.65
8	14.44	7.21	6.65	3.32
9	13.33	6.65	6.13	3.06
10	12.45	6.21	5.73	2.86
11	11.74	5.86	5.40	2.70
12	11.15	5.57	5.13	2.56
13	10.67	5.32	4.91	2.45
14	10.25	5.12	4.72	2.36
15	9.90	4.94	4.56	2.28
16	9.60	4.79	4.42	2.21
17	9.34	4.66	4.30	2.15
18	9.11	4.55	4.19	2.09
19	8.91	4.45	4.10	2.05
20	8.74	4.36	4.02	2.01
21	8.58	4.28	3.95	1.97
22	8.45	4.21	3.88	1.94
23	8.32	4.15	3.83	1.91
24	8.21	4.10	3.78	1.87
25	8.12	4.05	3.73	1.86

EACH $1,000 OF MORTGAGE X FACTOR = BLENDED PAYMENT.

Mortgage Payment Table   8.50% Rate

Number of Years	Paying monthly	Paying semi-monthly	Paying bi-weekly	Paying weekly
1	87.15	43.50	40.14	20.06
2	45.39	22.65	20.90	10.44
3	31.50	15.72	14.51	7.25
4	24.58	12.27	11.32	5.65
5	20.45	10.21	9.41	4.70
6	17.71	8.84	8.15	4.07
7	15.76	7.87	7.26	3.63
8	14.32	7.15	6.59	3.29
9	13.20	6.59	6.08	3.04
10	12.32	6.15	5.67	2.83
11	11.61	5.79	5.34	2.67
12	11.02	5.50	5.07	2.53
13	10.53	5.26	4.84	2.42
14	10.11	5.05	4.65	2.32
15	9.76	4.87	4.49	2.24
16	9.46	4.72	4.35	2.17
17	9.19	4.59	4.23	2.11
18	8.96	4.47	4.12	2.06
19	8.76	4.37	4.03	2.01
20	8.59	4.29	3.95	1.97
21	8.43	4.21	3.88	1.94
22	8.29	4.14	3.81	1.90
23	8.16	4.08	3.75	1.88
24	8.05	4.02	3.70	1.85
25	7.95	3.97	3.66	1.83

About the Author

George Boelcke, CCP is President of Vantage Consultants in Edmonton, Alberta and holds a degree in credit management. He is a member of the Credit Institute of Canada as well as the Association of Finance and Insurance Professionals.

With more than 25 years experience in the credit, banking and finance fields, George is one of the foremost experts on credit and debt in Canada. In addition to his weekly radio tips and frequent media appearances he is a contributing columnist for more than 21 North American newspapers.

George also facilitates team building, relationship, sales and personality types seminars throughout North America and Europe for firms ranging from Fortune 500 companies to small offices and church groups.

You can contact George through:george@vantageseminars.com

Order Form

#	Title	Investment per	Total amount
____	It's Your Money! Tools, Tips and Tricks to Borrow Smarter	$19.95	_____
____	The Canadian Financial Nightmare CD	$19.95/set of 4	_____
____	Colorful Personalities – Discover Your Personality Type Through the Power of Colors	$19.95	_____
____	Colorful Personalities – Audio CD	$9.95	_____
____	The Colors of Leadership & Mgmt.	$6.95	_____
____	The Colors of Parent & Child Dynamics	$6.95	_____
____	The Colors of Sales & Customers	$6.95	_____
____	The Colors of Relationships	$6.95	_____
____	Colors Tools for Christians	$6.95	_____

Tax & shipping – No Charge

Total amount: _____

Name: _____

Address: _____

City: _____ Pr.: _____ PC: _____

E-mail: _____

Payment enclosed by: ____cheque ____cash ____M.O.

Or Visa/MC: _____/_____/_____/_____ Exp date:___/___

Order by: Fax: (780) 432 5613 Web: www.yourmoneybook.com
E-mail: george@vantageseminars.com
Mail: Box 4080 Edmonton, AB, T6E 4S8